Mastering the Art of Display: A Comprehensive Guide to Picture Framing

Kenleighx Q. Downs

All rights reserved. Copyright © 2023 Kenleighx Q. Downs

COPYRIGHT © 2023 Kenleighx Q. Downs

All rights reserved.

No part of this book must be reproduced, stored in a retrieval system, or shared by any means, electronic, mechanical, photocopying, recording, or otherwise, without written permission from the publisher.

Every precaution has been taken in the preparation of this book; still the publisher and author assume no responsibility for errors or omissions. Nor do they assume any liability for damages resulting from the use of the information contained herein.

Legal Notice:

This book is copyright protected and is only meant for your individual use. You are not allowed to amend, distribute, sell, use, quote or paraphrase any of its part without the written consent of the author or publisher.

Introduction

Have you ever admired a beautifully framed picture and wondered how it was done? Picture framing is not only a practical skill but also a creative outlet that allows you to showcase and preserve your cherished artwork, photographs, and memories. In this comprehensive guide, designed specifically for complete beginners, we will take you on a journey to discover the art and craft of picture framing.

We start with the basics, exploring the essential tools and materials you'll need to embark on your framing journey. From the mitre block and tenon saw for precise cutting to the hand mitre saw for more intricate designs, we'll guide you through the selection and use of these tools. Additionally, we introduce you to the strap clamp and corner clamp, indispensable tools for ensuring sturdy and precise frame assembly. You'll also learn about the mount and matt cutting tools and the versatile kraft knife that will help you achieve professional-looking results.

Understanding the materials used in framing is crucial, and we dedicate a section to delve into the different components. You'll discover the various types of moulding available, allowing you to select the perfect frame style for your artwork. We also introduce you to mountboard or mattboard, essential for creating a border around your pictures. Glass, an important element for protecting your artwork, is also covered in this guide, along with additional materials that enhance the framing process.

Once you're equipped with the necessary knowledge, we guide you through the process of sourcing moulding, offering valuable tips and resources to help you find quality materials for your frames. From local suppliers to online options, you'll learn how to navigate the market and make informed choices.

With the foundational knowledge in place, we dive into the practical aspect of making picture frames. We provide step-by-step instructions and expert tips for frame assembly, ensuring that you achieve seamless corners and sturdy constructions. Learn how to make adjustments, create tight joints, and use techniques such as making good and taping up to achieve professional results.

As you gain confidence and experience, we explore semi-professional framing, which offers advanced techniques and considerations for those looking to take their framing skills to the next level. Discover insider tips on making frames, assembling them with precision, and adding finishing touches to enhance their appearance.

Moreover, we recognize that your newfound skills in picture framing may open doors to selling your creations. We offer guidance on promoting yourself and your framing services, helping you navigate the world of entrepreneurship and showcasing your talent to potential customers.

Throughout the guide, we touch upon various aspects of framing, from color theory and design considerations to conservation framing and archival techniques. We aim to provide a well-rounded understanding of the art and science behind picture framing, empowering you to create beautiful, professional-quality frames for your own enjoyment or as a potential business venture.

Picture framing is an art form that combines creativity, precision, and craftsmanship. By following the steps and techniques outlined in this guide, you will develop the skills and knowledge needed to create stunning frames that showcase your artwork in the best possible light. So, let's dive in and unlock the world of picture framing for complete beginners. Get ready to bring your pictures to life and embark on an exciting and rewarding framing journey.

Contents

HOBBY AND SMALL SCALE FRAMING 1
    INTRODUCTION 2
    Mitre block and tenon saw 3
    Hand Mitre Saw 5
    Strap clamp or corner clamp - or both 5
    Mount, Matt(Card Surround) Cutting Tool 5
    Kraft Knife 7
    Additional Tools 8
    Moulding 9
    Mountboard/Mattboard 9
    Glass 9
    Additional materials 9
    SOURCING YOUR MOULDING 11
    MAKING THE FRAMES 13

SEMI PROFESSIONAL FRAMING 53
    INTRODUCTION 53
    MAKING PICTURE FRAMES 109
    ASSEMBLING THE FRAME 158
    Making Good 161
    Taping Up 161
    Fixing, Hangings & Frame Furniture 163
    SELLING YOURSELF AND YOUR FRAMING 166

ASPECTS OF FRAMING 177

ONE
HOBBY AND SMALL SCALE FRAMING

INTRODUCTION

You do not need to have expensive equipment to make a frame, and this section i s for those who want to make picture frames on a small scale without the expensive tools and equipment required for a professional or semi professional framer. I would however stress that the same basic framing rules apply in that you want to produce a frame of high quality, especially if you are an artist (professional or amateur) who sells works of art. The framing must enhance your work both through appearance and quality. How many art club exhibitions have you seen with competent and attractive pictures ruined by bad framing? (Consequently how many lost sales!)

The Complete Picture Framer is divided into clearly marked sections, all aspects of framing explained in easy to follow step by step instructions, so it is recommended that even if you are only making hobby frames, you read and refer back to the other chapters in the "Professional" section i.e. making frames, stretching canvas, tapestries, wash line mounts, etc., as all the processes, tips and advice contained therein remains the same whether applying to making one frame or one hundred.

As with other sections in the book, I will deal firstly with tools and workspace then the framing construction and finally the finish.

TOOLS AND WORKSPACE

The only part of the framing process that involves any dusty mess is the moulding cutting, which is performed with a saw. Other than that, a well protected table will be perfectly adequate. A board of half inch ply 4 feet by 3 feet would be ideal with a sheet between table and board - you can then cut and trim without fear of ruining the family heirloom!

There follows a list of tools that will be essential to your framing:

Mitre block and tenon saw

This is a beech wood block into which the moulding fits. The tenon saw is held in 45 degree splits on both sides which guide it while cutting. This is the most basic and traditional means of mitre cutting.

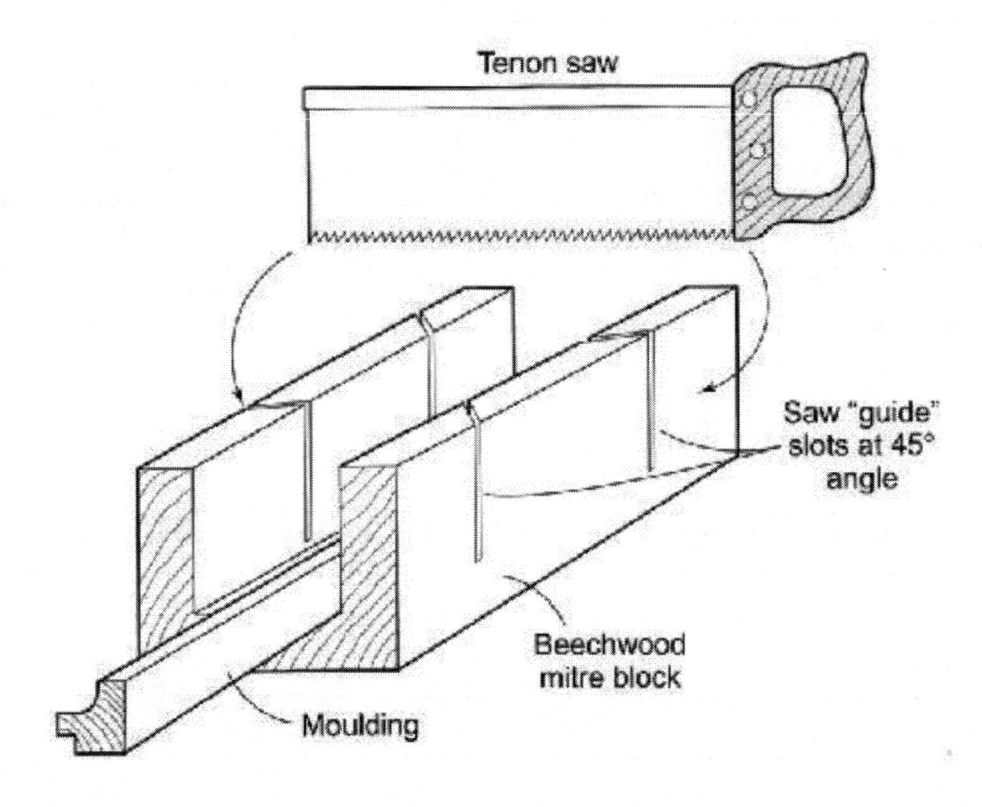

Mitre block and tenon saw

Hand Mitre Saw

This is a saw built into a light metal framework which holds the saw and has vari-angle settings. These range in price from £30 to £100 and would be your preferred option.

Strap clamp or corner clamp - or both

A strap clamp is a four corner stay held by a string which is placed around the frame to hold it whilst the glue dries. (See Equipping Workshop in section II for more detailed explanation and diagram.)

The corner clamp is a small screw clamp that holds two pieces of moulding whilst you pin and glue. Tool shops sell a variety of straps and clamps and you can spend as little as £20 or as much as £100 but you will definitely need some form of clamp/strap. If unsure go for a strap.

Mount, Matt(Card Surround) Cutting Tool

If you are going to cut a bevelled opening in your mount, you must have a mount cutting tool of some description, for straight, circular or oval mounts. These vary in price from £20 to £100 but if this is beyond your budget, remember you can buy ready cut mounts of standard sizes in art shops but without one of the patent devices, you will not get a mount with that attractive professional bevelled cut/finish.

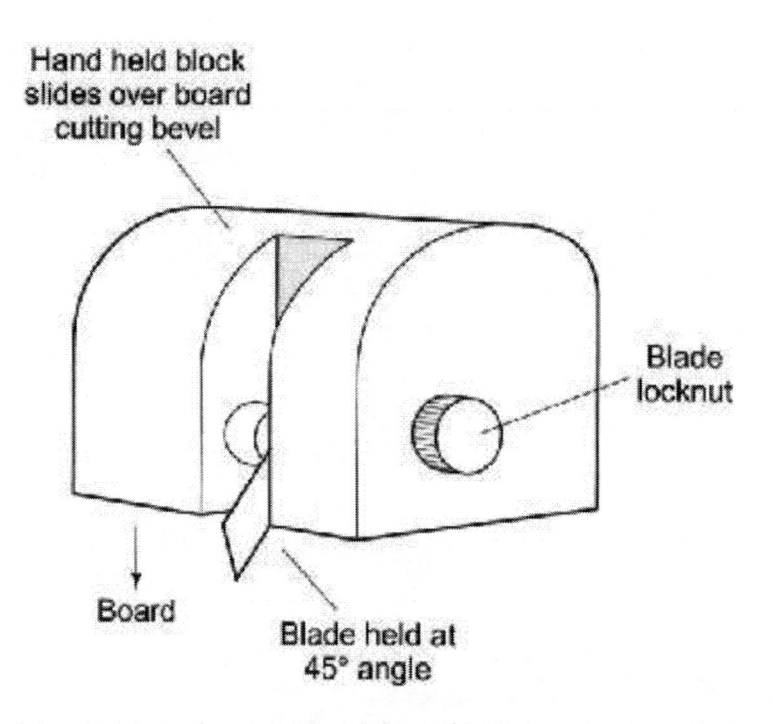

Mount-cutting block

Kraft Knife

The Stanley knife type is best and a straight edge. Buy a good quality straight edge WITH FINGER PROTECTION. Kraft knives are very sharp and can inflict fearful wounds. Please heed this.

Additional Tools

You will need the following tools to make the frames but you will probably already have these in your tool box:

Panel pin hammer

Small wood block approximately 40mm x 40mm x 60mm (1.5" x 1.5" x 3")

Countersink

Accurate set square (to check angles and mitres for accuracy)

1 metre (1 foot) measure/rule (accurate)

Pencils

Bradawl (for boring holes)

Drill (either hand or electric)

Fine drill bits (the thickness of your panel pins)

Scissors

Pliers (blunt ended and pointed varieties)

Selection of artists brushes (No. 2 & No. 4)

Glass cutter (2mm) (Depending on your confidence)

Clean Dusters

MATERIALS NEEDED

Moulding
This can be from a variety of sources - old frames (however be careful if you intend to utilize old frames from markets or auctions of woodworm. You do not want to introduce woodworm to your home or worse still, someone else's!). Lengths can be obtained from a picture framing shop, moulding wholesaler or from DIY stores and builders merchants.

Mountboard/Mattboard
Card for decorative effect - from Craft shops, art shops or framing retailers/wholesalers.

Backing - thin (2mm) hardboard, MDF board, foam core board - from framers or Craft suppliers.

Glass
You require 2mm picture framing glass either clear, non reflecting or UV protecting which can be obtained from a framer or glazier's shop. The glass can be brought ready cut to size (ask the Glazier to de-edge it for your safety - at least until you are confident in handling it) or by the sheet and cut it yourself.

Additional materials
Brown gum strip paper (30mm/2"wide rolls)
Masking tape (25mm/1"wide rolls)
Double sided tape (20mm wide rolls)
PVA wood glue (normal, NOT waterproof)
Artists' acrylic paints (for touching up and decorating)
Panel pins - from 20mm/3-4" to 40mm/1.5" to 25mm/1"

Rings or screw eyes
Wire/string for hanging
Glass cleaning liquid (non smear variety)

SOURCING YOUR MOULDING

First you will have to find a source for your moulding. Here are a few suggestions:

a) Moulding Wholesalers

These companies are the Professional picture framer's trade suppliers but most now have a trade counter where they sell to the general public - at a price!

The Professionals get their discount through bulk buying so if you have a friend who makes frames or you belong to an art club, think about one person buying the moulding for a group thereby benefiting from a bulk discount. This could apply to all your materials.

b) DIY stores or from Picture Framers.

Both of the above will often provide a cutting service, leaving you to assemble the frames. This will get you a perfect mitre and can be a very good idea.

c) Builders' Merchants

Builders' Merchants carry a range of moulding's used in the carpentry trade. Some of the moulding may be ornate architrave or coving and may not be rebated (the recess in moulding designed to take the picture). This can be overcome by attaching a batten to form a rebate (see paragraph "Cutting, Assembling and Decorating" in "Making the Frame). Plain wood frames are ideal if you want to decorate your own frames.

d) Second hand frames

From junk shops, skips, markets - there are always frames around old pictures that have been disposed of as fashions change. These can be great fun to simply renovate and re-use but remember the warning I mentioned before and stress again - old frames can be infested with woodworm. Watch for the tell tale holes and the sawdust like powder that indicates activity.

MAKING THE FRAMES

As mentioned in the introduction, I strongly recommend that you read the relevant chapters in the Professional section of the book as the same procedures apply except that you will be using hand tools instead of the machinery. However, you may find the explanations given of use.

Measuring the picture

Your first task is to decide the size of your frame - is your picture to be close framed or framed with a m ount? If the answer is the former, the size of the picture will decide the size of your frame. Allow a loose fit (for expansion and contraction of the picture) and make the frame slightly larger than the picture. You do not want to make a frame and discover the picture does not fit - trust me, it happens!

Your other option is a mounted picture, that is, a picture with a decorative surround, usually behind glass. For this, measure the picture then decide on the width of the mount. The balance and size of the mount is vital to prevent the presentation looking out of kilter, unbalanced or crushed into the frame, the latter b eing a common fault when pictures have been fitted into an existing frame and the mount trimmed to allow for the incompatible dimensions. Having decided on the mount dimensions, ADD them to the picture size, not forgetting to double the width and the height, i.e. a 3" mount will add 6 inches to the length and to the width.

Cutting, Assembling and Decorating the Frame

If you are using decorative moulding from a Builders Merchants and require to form a rebate, buy some 10mm x 40mm (3/8" x 1¾") batten and glue it under the moulding, secured by masking tape until the glue has dried (normally this takes about 24 hours).

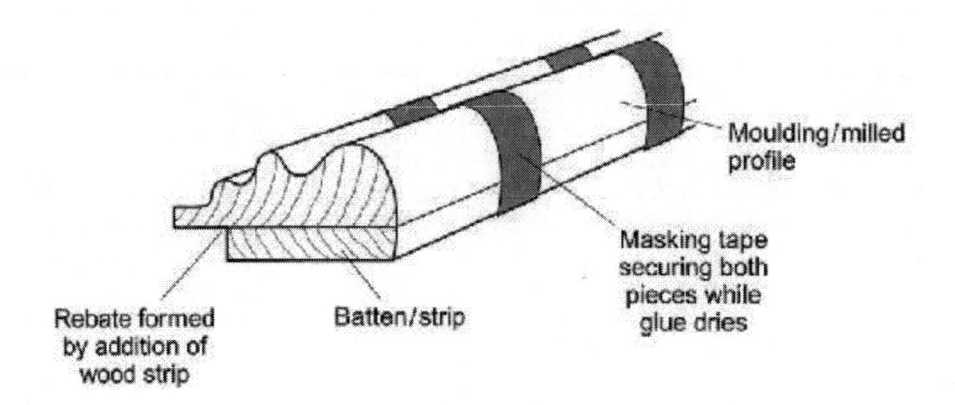

Moulding and batten

Take your length of moulding and offer it up to the jig or saw base then trim off the end to 45 degrees. This will give you your first mitre. Measure and mark off the length on the inside of the rebate and carefully cut the moulding to the mark. This will give you your first length.

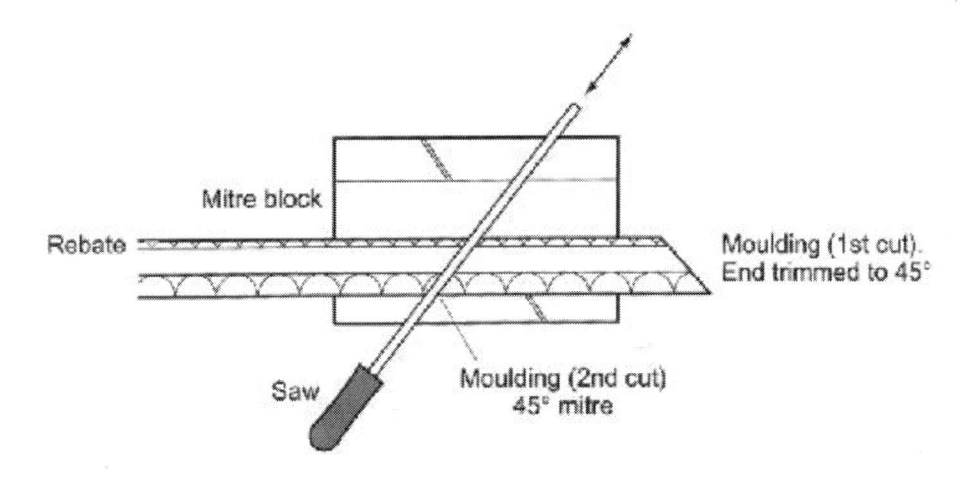

Trimming moulding (1st & 2nd cuts)

Trim the moulding again to get the next mitre

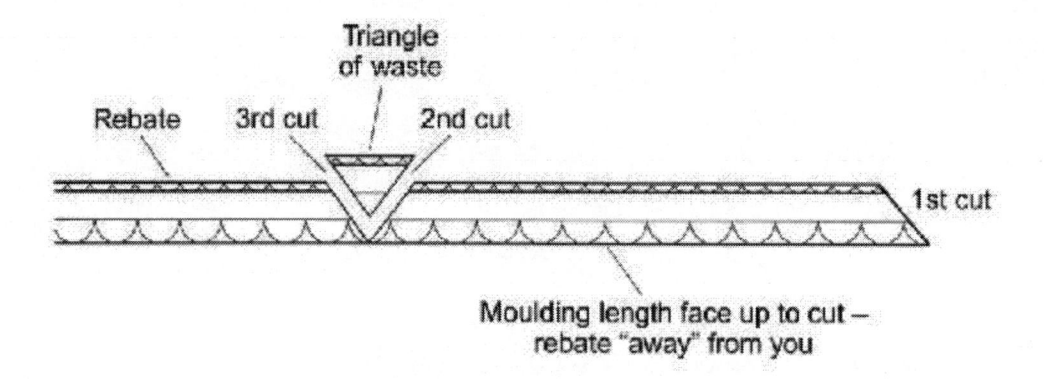

Rebate   3rd cut   Triangle of waste   2nd cut   1st cut

Moulding length face up to cut – rebate "away" from you

First length cut

To get the second identical length, place the moulding beside the first length and mark off exactly where to cut. Cut the second length. Your two lengths must be exact to ensure your frame is square!

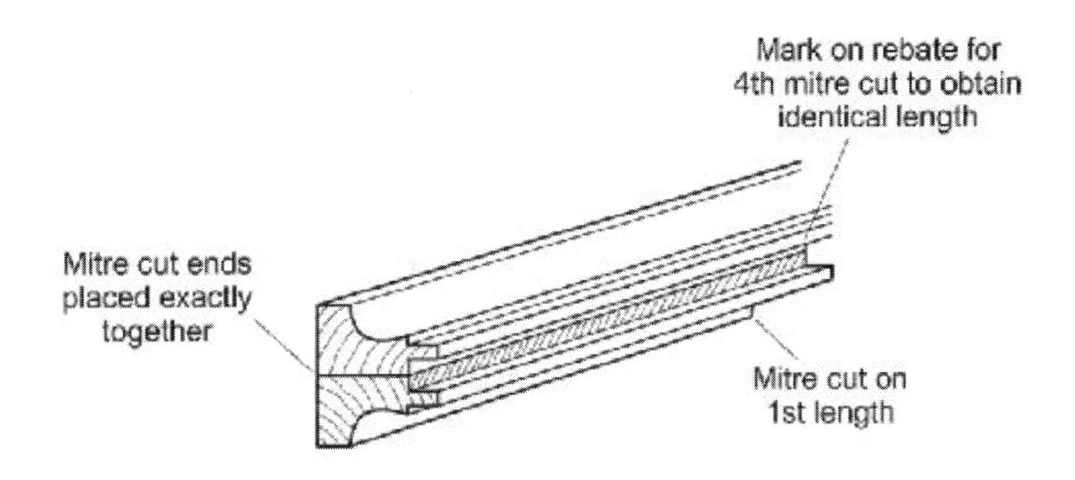

Mark on rebate for 4th mitre cut to obtain identical length

Mitre cut ends placed exactly together

Mitre cut on 1st length

Mitre-cut ends placed exactly together

Repeat the process for the second pair of lengths/sides. You should now have the four sides of your frame. With the set square, check your mitres are accurate.

String clamp method

Open up your string clamp, larger than the frame. Place the four sides of moulding on the bench and adjust the string clamp around the frame, pull tight and double check all is well. This is where you must be self critical. If the mitres do not close together perfectly, re-do them because you will never get a perfect joint with inaccurate cuts. Once satisfied, release the string clamp and carefully remove one length. Smear a thin layer of glue to both ends then carefully replace. Repeat with the opposite length so that all four joints will now be glued. Close up the string clamp under tension. Once this has been done, do not fiddle with it as you will impair the glue joint. (PVA wood glue when dried under pressure will form a joint stronger than the wood itself.). Leave the frame to dry for a MINIMUM of 24 hours before removing the clamp.

Once the frame has dried and been removed from the clamp, it will have to be pinned on each mitre. Working in rotation, pre drill a small hole then tap in your panel pin and countersink slightly. The countersink hole can be filled and touched up later but if you are very neat, you can leave them as being on the side or spine of the moulding, they will not show.

Tap in panel pin

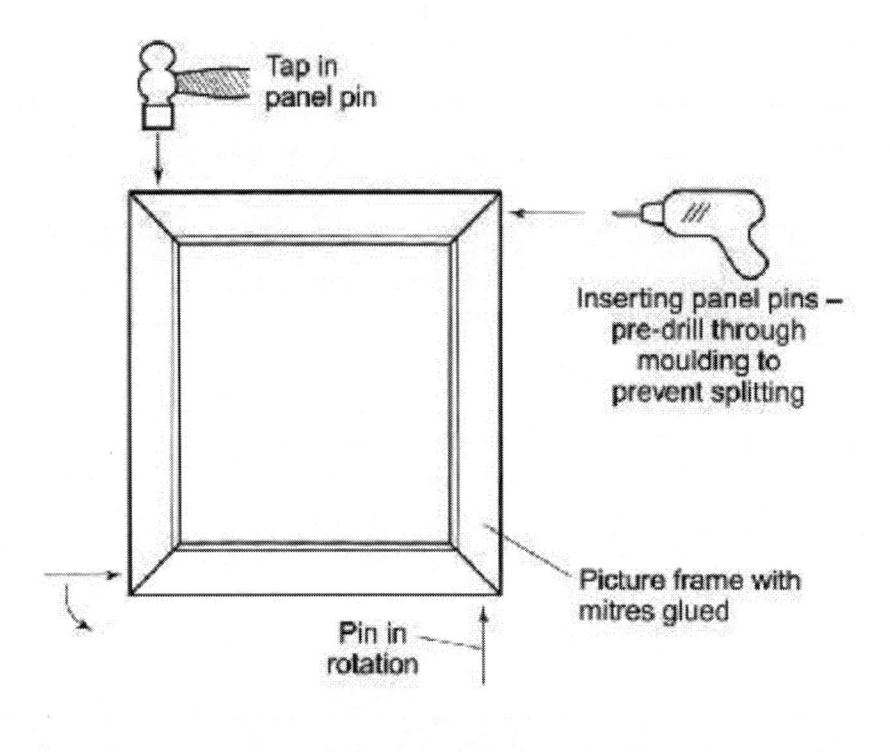

Inserting panel pins – pre-drill through moulding to prevent splitting

Picture frame with mitres glued

Pin in rotation

Drill and pin corners

Corner Clamps

If you are using a corner clamp, insert a length and width of moulding and screw down the clamps to hold the two pieces. Check that they are a snug and accurate fit. Remove one length, apply a thin smear of glue over the joint and replace in clamp. Drill and pin the corner and leave to dry.

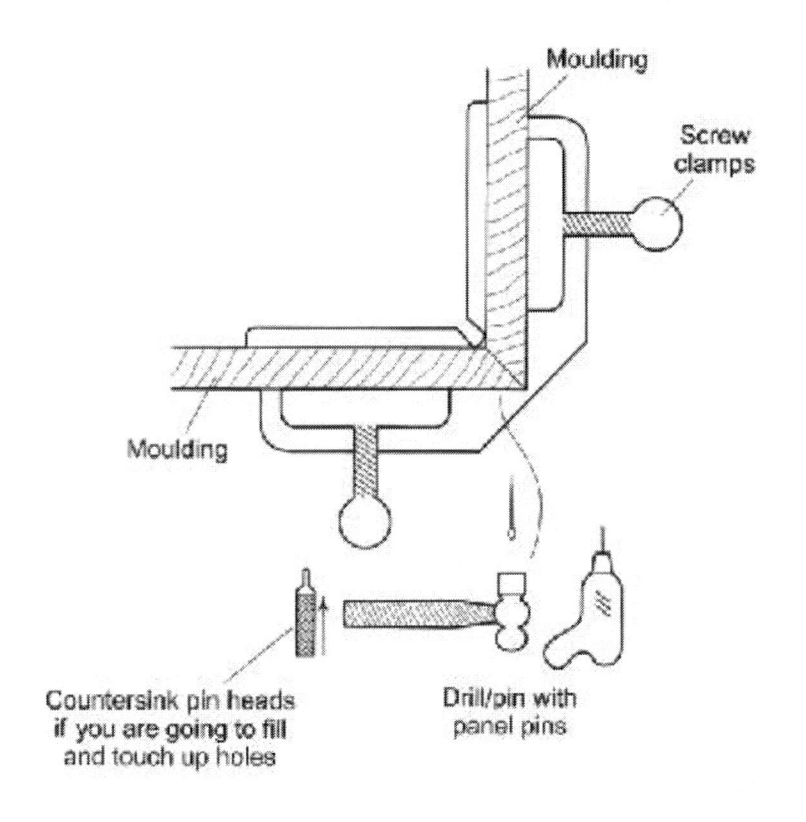

Moulding

Screw clamps

Moulding

Countersink pin heads if you are going to fill and touch up holes

Drill/pin with panel pins

Corner/mitre clamp

Now take the second pair of lengths and insert them into the clamp and repeat the process, making sure that they are in the same way as the first pair so that the two halves of your frame marry up! Once the pair of "Ls" you have made are dry, fix together in the clamp using the same method.

If you only have one clamp, it is worth taking time over the joints to allow them to dry under pressure - 12 hours is sufficient. You will now have your made up frame.

If you are using commercially produced moulding that is pre decorated, your joint will have to be left. You cannot touch up the face of this type of moulding; you are likely to give it a 'botched' appearance. The quality of your mitre joint is thus very important. Take care and with practice you will get a good joint. On the commercially produced moulding, it might be wise to have a framer trim it to size for you. His guillotine will produce an almost invisible joint. On the other hand, if you are using plane wood moulding you intend to decorate, (I would recommend this for the Hobby Framer), you can fill the mitres before painting and decorating.

Decorating the Frame

The simplest way to decorate your frame is to use your acrylic paints to paint the frame usually a colour that complements and enhances the picture. However there are three basic ways to decorate your frame.
1. Stain the wood with wood stain then varnish
2. Paint the frame with acrylic paint (I don't recommend anyone to use paints that might contain toxic solvents. They are not good for you, so avoid them.)
3. Ornament the frame. There are limitless ideas for decorating the frame with all kinds of objects and textures, for example a seascape might be enhanced by a frame with seashells glued to it. There are various cold cure

modelling clays which can be used to model objects to stick to the frame such as leaves or flowers.

Don't be afraid to experiment. You will have disasters but nothing ventured. ......!

MAKING THE FRAME

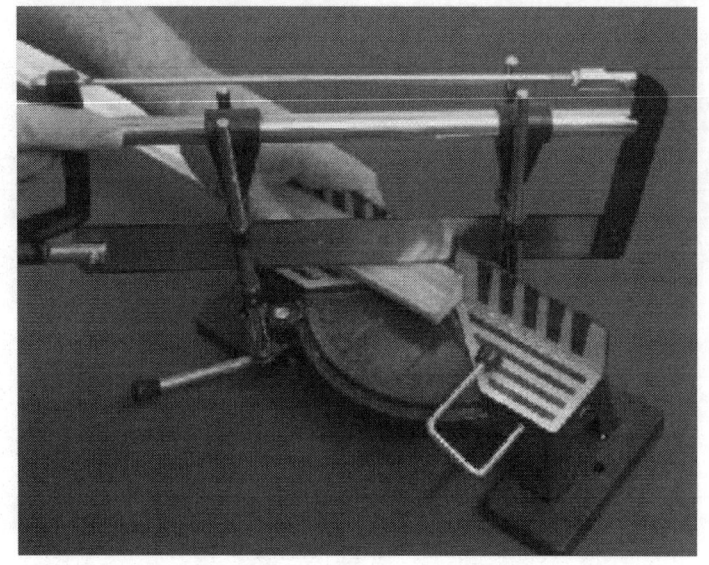

1. Trim off end of moulding with mitre saw

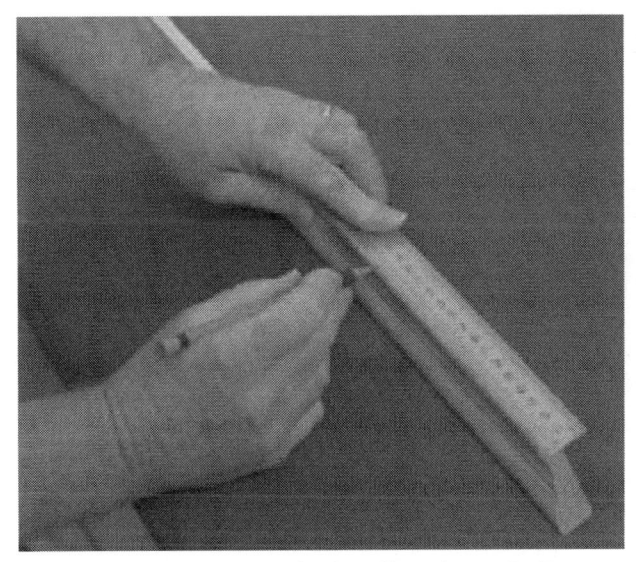

2. Measure and mark the first length for mitre cut.

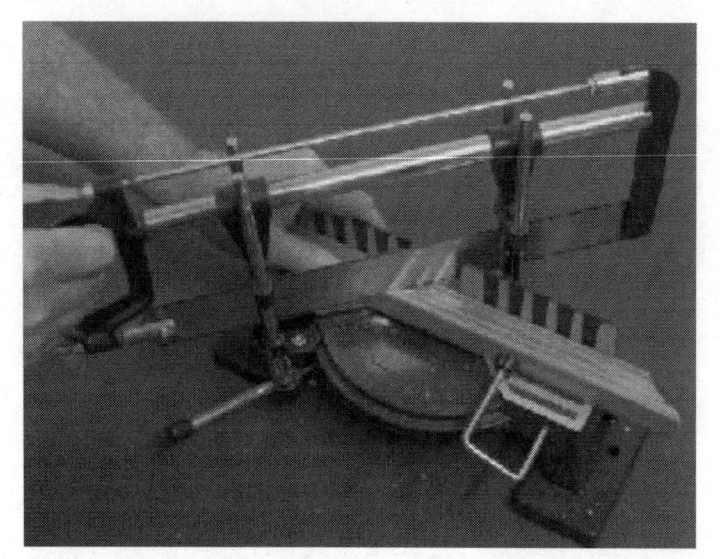

3. Cut second mitre.

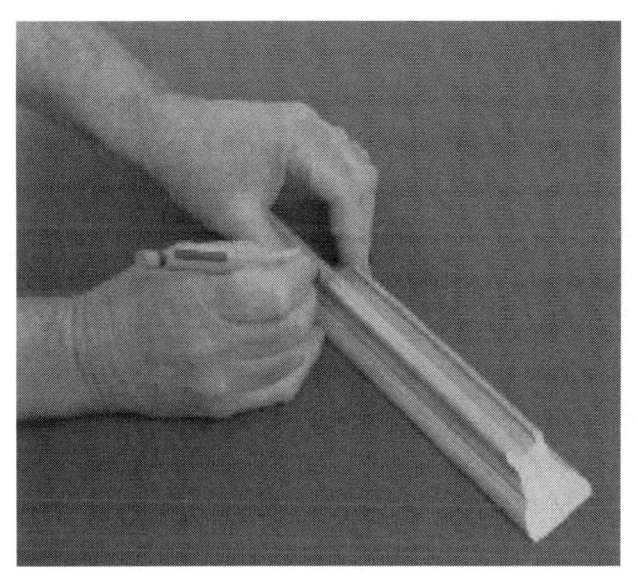

4. Using first length measure off and mark second length to get perfect match.

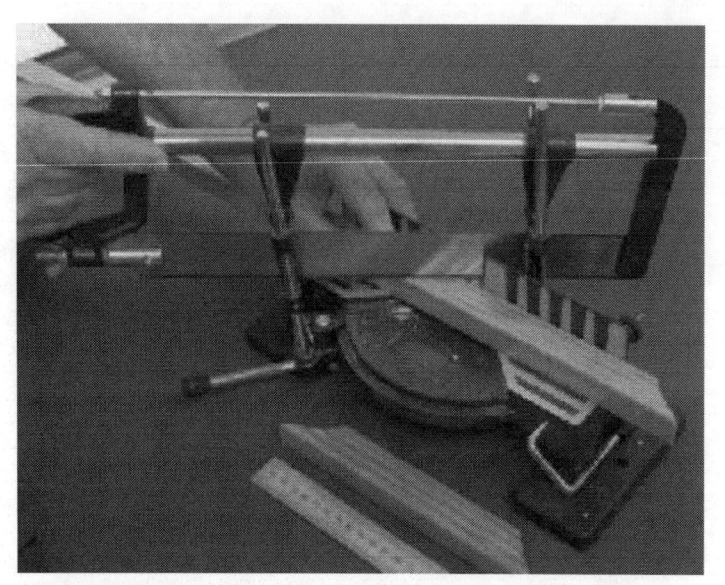

5. Cut second length - repeat process for other two sides.

6. The four sides of the frame cut and ready for assembly.

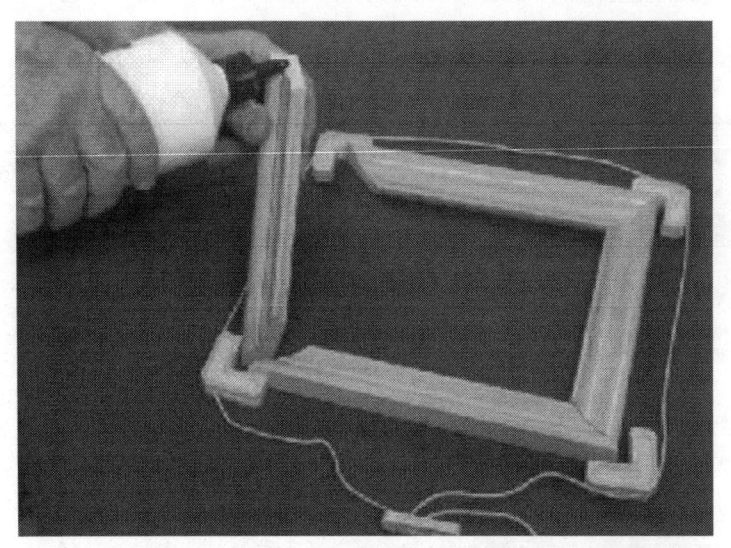

7. Arrange the string clamp a thin layer of PVA interior wood glue on mitres.

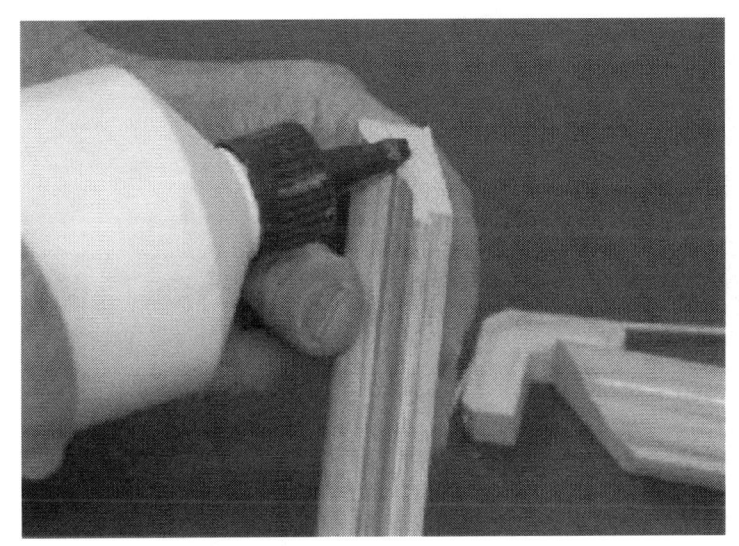

8. Spread a thin layer of glue.

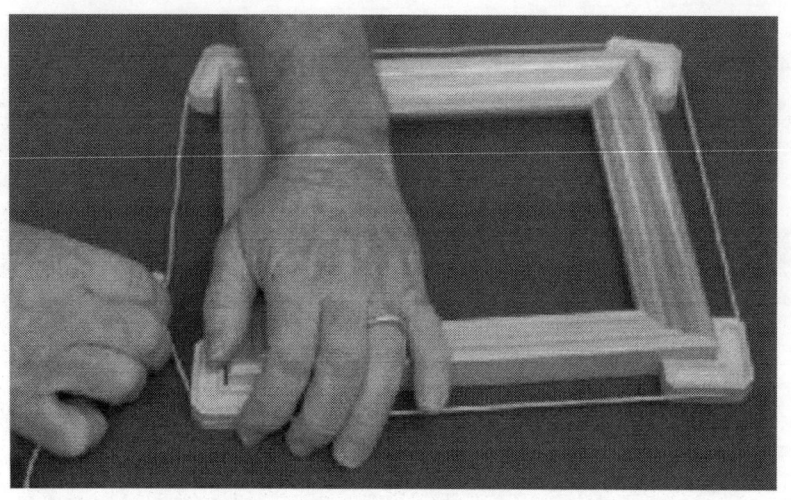

9. Adjust the string clamp.

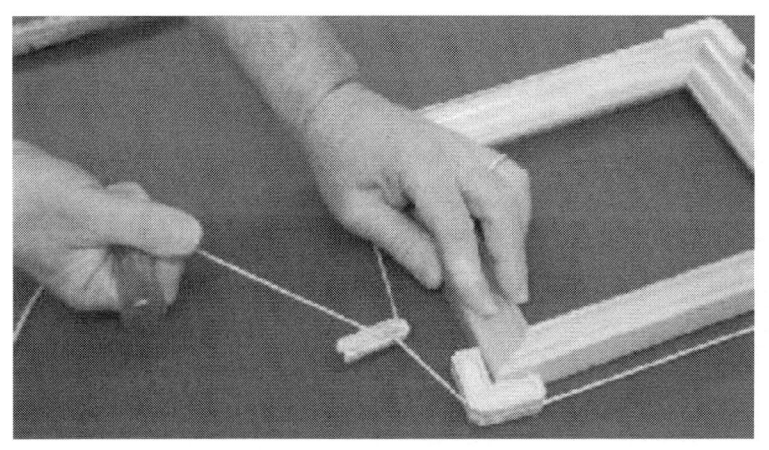

10. Tension the clamp to ensure frame dries under pressure - wrap the string around a screwdriver or other implement/moulding off-cut to increase your leverage.

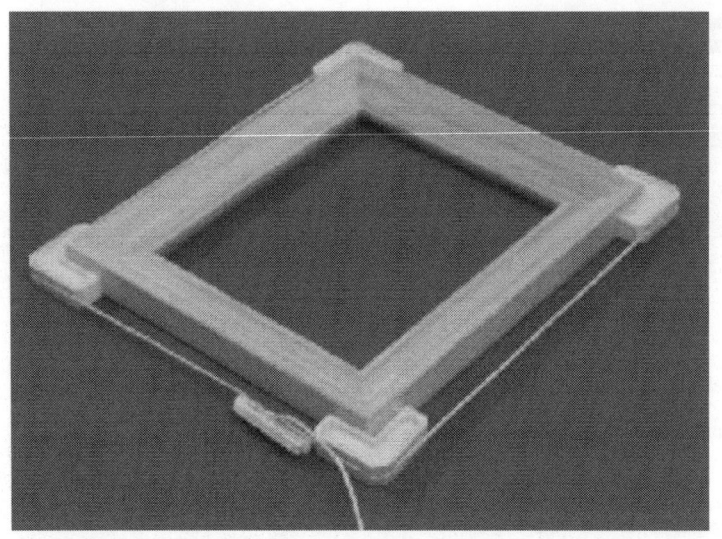

11. Frame clamped and left overnight for glue to dry.

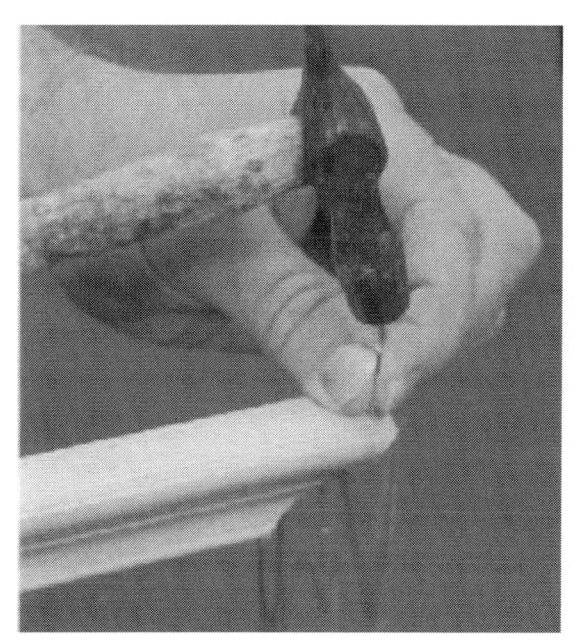

12. Pre-drill and tap in panel pins (always work in rotation).

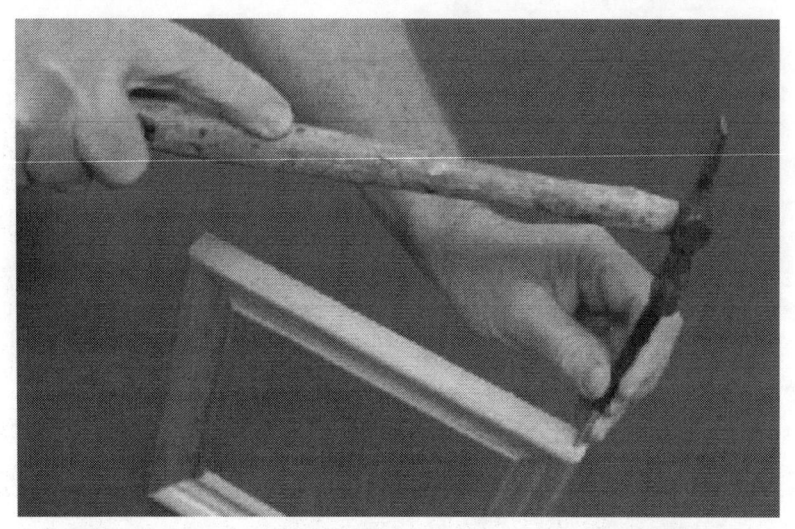

13. Using centre punch make sure panel pins are flush or just below the surface - and fill the holes to mask the pins (optional)

FINISHING THE FRAME

Finishing a basic frame
If the picture to be framed requires only a simple frame, i.e. with nothing more than a frame around it, you can now check that it fits. If you are happy with the fit, place the picture atop of your chosen backing board - 2mm hardboard, MDF, Foam core, Pulp board - and trace the outline of the picture onto the board. Cut out with the Stanley knife and insert both picture and board into the frame, pin in place and tape up. (See pinning and taping methods given below).

Finishing a frame with mount /matt and glass
The mount (a coloured card surrounding picture) is designed to enhance the picture and separate it from the glass with its attendant condensation problem (especially important in Britain's wet climate).

You can buy your mount board from an art shop, Craft shop, bulk buy it from Framing Wholesalers or buy it from Framers who will also cut it for you, if you want. There are also ready cut mounts of standard size that you can buy from art shops and some Framers.

To cut your mount takes patience, requiring practice and great care to achieve the result you want which is a straight, even surround with a bevelled edge on the picture opening.

There are several patent cutting systems for the Hobby Framer. The simplest I know is a DEXTER MATT CUTTER, a simple metal block which holds a blade at 45 degrees. You place a straight edge between two predetermined points and slide the Dexter along. Repeated on all sides, this produces a very professional finish.

You can also cut out the aperture using a craft knife. The problem here is that it will be a straight cut not a bevel cut and will not look as good.

The basic system to follow is first cut out the card to the OUTER dimension. Then on the reverse side, using pencil and rule, work out where the INNER cut is to be. Having established this, make four fine pinhol es in the corners. Turn the board good side up and cut out your aperture using your pin holes as guidelines. If you are using one of the Patent Devices, follow the instructions as each has varying advice. For a Double or Triple Mount, follow the above procedure, first marking and cutting the card to produce the various 'layers' of mount then fix them together with great care - ensuring they are straight and accurate - with a strip of doub le sided tape along and behind the top border.

If cutting on face prick 4 pinholes from back through each intersect to mark face

Mount board cut to exact outer dimension

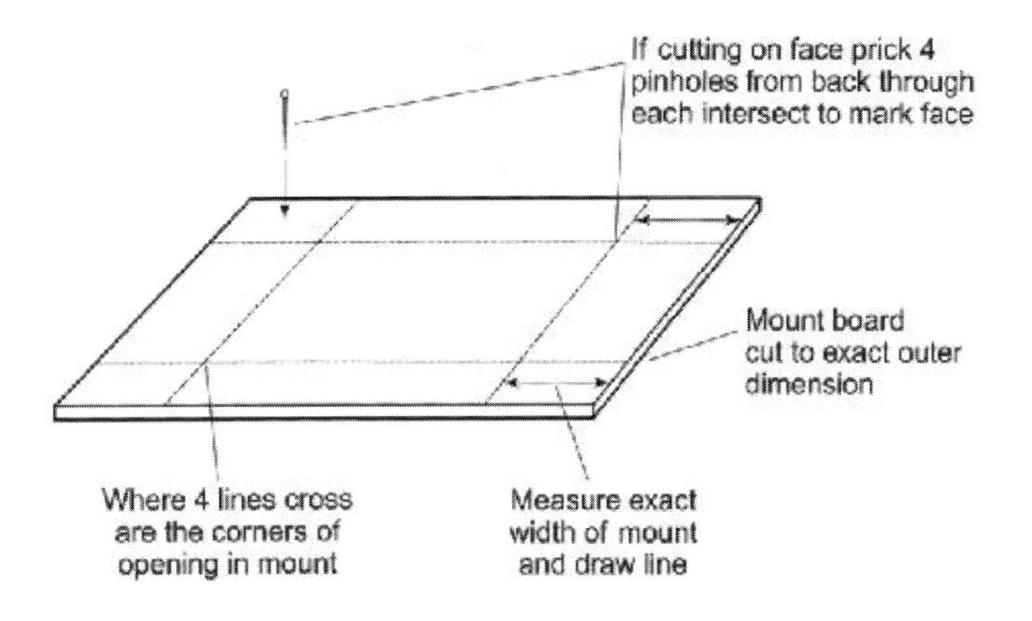

Where 4 lines cross are the corners of opening in mount

Measure exact width of mount and draw line

Cutting mount board

HAND CUTTING MOUNT

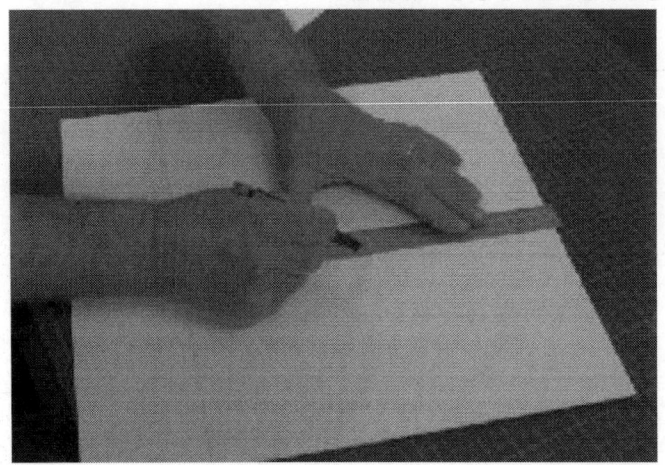

1 & 2. Measure and mark outer dimensions of mount board on rear surface. This must be very accurate.

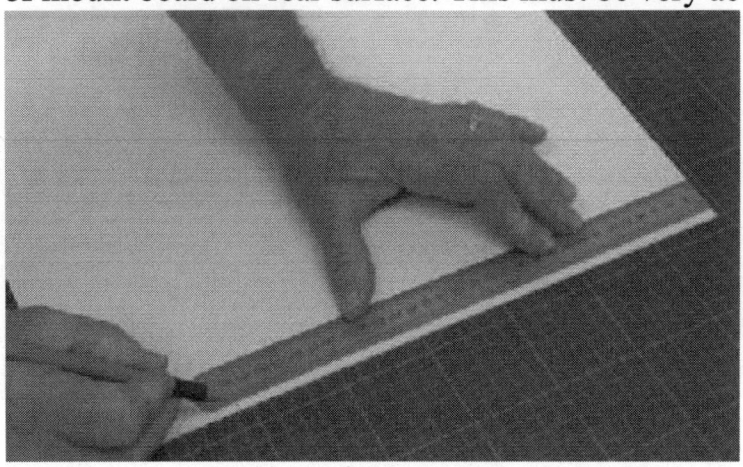

3. Carefully trim board to size.

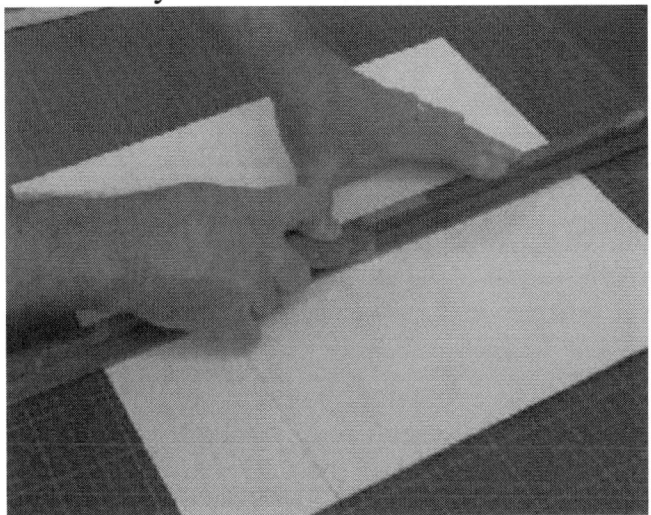

4. Using dividers mark out the width of the mount (i.e. the outer to the inner cut which will surround the picture).

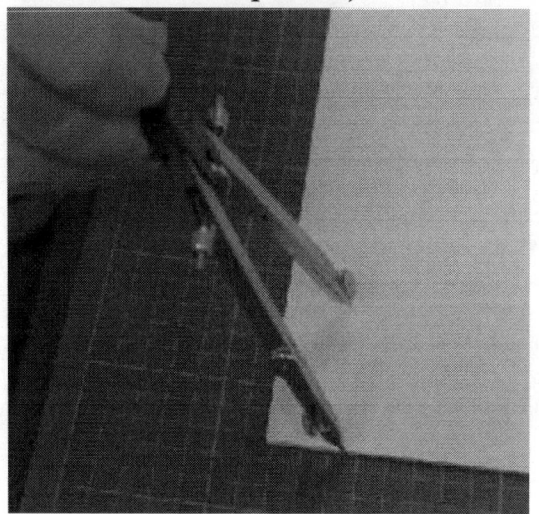

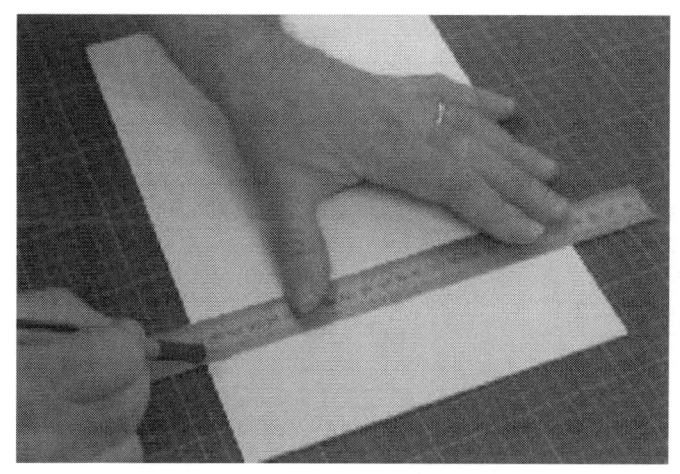

5. Mark/connect with fine pencil lines

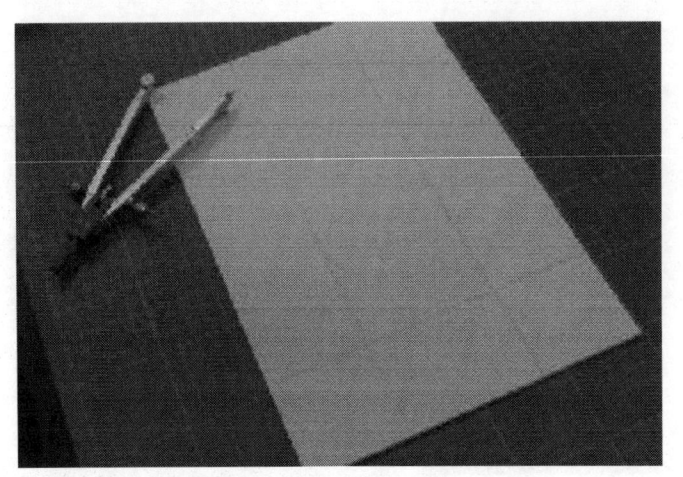

6. The mount board ready for 'bevel' cutting (I always use dividers to reduce the risk of mistakes).

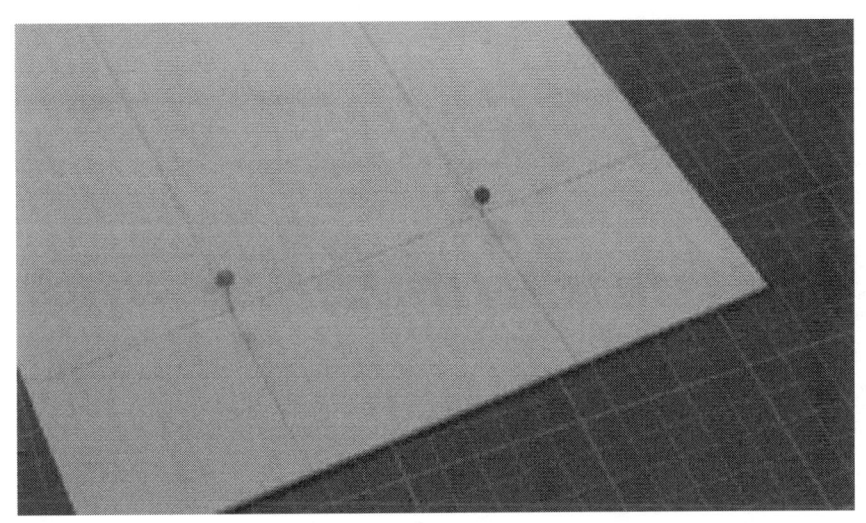

7. Using a fine pin mark the four corners to show where to cut on the mount board face (this is ONLY if you are using a cutting block that works from the face, I.e. Dexter matt cutter). If you have the variety that cuts from the rear, this is unnecessary.

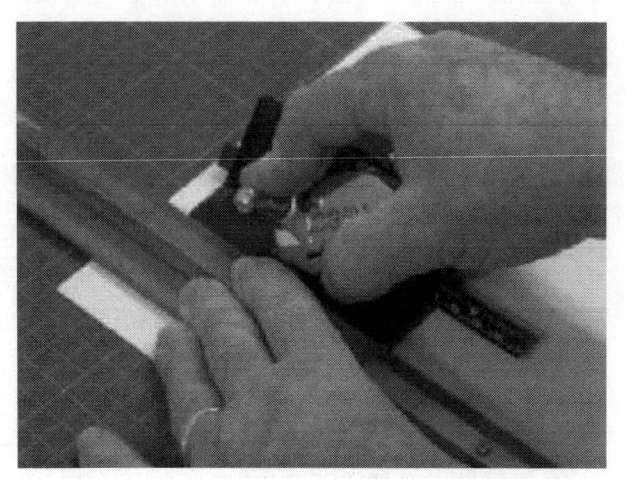

8. Cut out the centre using your lines as guides.
N.B. I have used an inexpensive patent cutter for this. You can use a Kraft knife but you will find the results far from satisfactory.

9. The mounts/matts cut and ready.

For more complex mounts and wash line mounts, please refer to the appropriate chapters in the professional section.

Glass and Glass Cutting

It goes without saying that glass must be handled with care - it can be dangerous.

I would strongly recommend that you have your local glazier cut your glass to size for you. Also ask him to DE-EDGE it to make it safe to handle. If, however, you want to cut your own, you will require a good glass cutter and a single layer of blanket on your cutting table.

Practice your cutting. The secret is to remember, firstly, run the wheel over the cut line just ONCE, exerting the right pressure so that the wheel SINGS as it runs. Once you have scoured the glass, take the sheet to the edge of the table, placing the scour line JUST past the edge and apply a quick, firm push.

Remember: nothing violent. If scoured correctly, it will snap cleanly along the line. Please be patient with this. Glass cutting is much like riding a bicycle. It takes time to perfect but once mastered, never forgotten. (Don't forget to wear eye protection to guard against flying splinters/shards/)

Backing

This is the final ingredient of making your frame. The finish on the back is very important, especially if you are framing your artwork to sell.

The easiest method is to use the sheet of glass as your template, tracing it onto your backing sheet which is then cut out with your Stanley knife and straight edge. (It is a good idea, if not essential, to place a sheet of card under the board to be cut to act as a cushion for the knife, also to have a special cutting board of 1cm thick ply which when damaged can be inverted and eventually replaced.

Assembling the Frame

Having cut and prepared the component parts, first clean the glass in the frame on both sides ensuring you have no smears and no dust. Cover with the backing and prepare the picture. This will entail fixing it to the mount using double sided tape. Make sure the picture is straight and only fix along the top edge. To prevent cockling, the picture should be able to expand and contract so by fixing on one edge only it leaves 3 edges for movement. Place the mounted picture in the frame, again checking for dust. (If you have a vacuum cleaner with an extension hose and CLEAN brush, use this to vacuum the glass to remove dust.)

Pinning

Now pin the back in place using the following method. Take the small wooden block mentioned in "Tools" and put it against the moulding. Place a 20mm panel pin up against the rebate and hold in place - thumb round block, fingers on backing, one finger on the pin - and with the hammer tap in of its length. Repeat near each corner.

With the contents now held, turn over and re-check once again that the glass is free of dust on the interior and that the picture & mount are straight. If you are unsure of your judgement, use dividers to check accuracy. Once you are happy that all is as it should be, (**remember:** be critical!) continue pinning the back, inserting panel pins every 80mm/3" all round, keeping them evenly spaced and neat. The idea of the wood block is that it absorbs impact shock from the hammer to protect the frame.

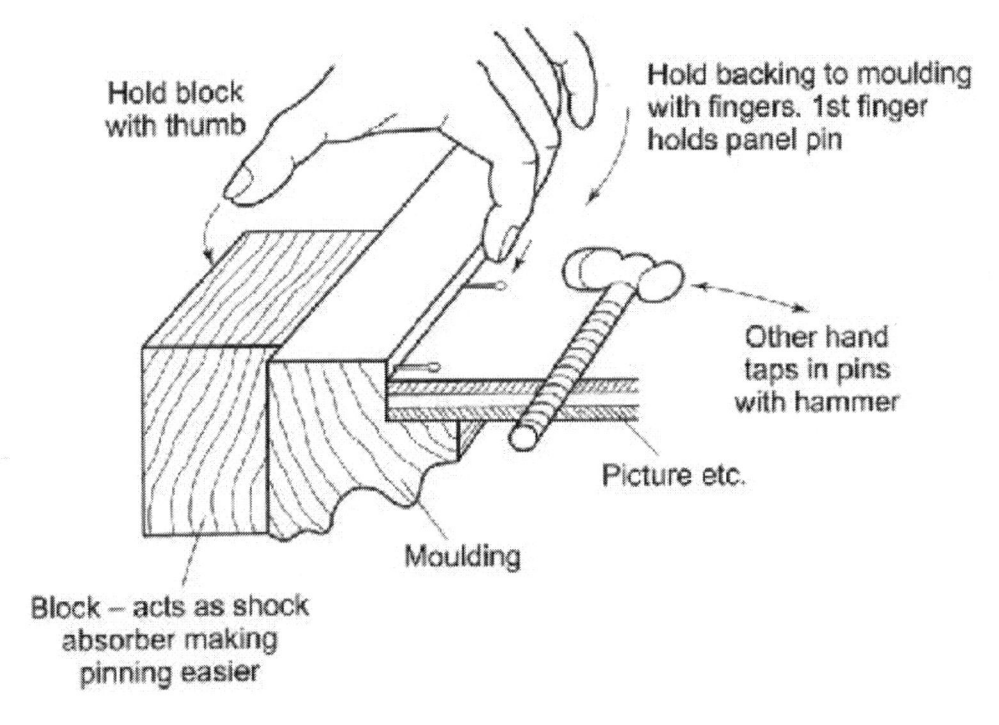

Hold block with thumb

Hold backing to moulding with fingers. 1st finger holds panel pin

Other hand taps in pins with hammer

Picture etc.

Moulding

Block – acts as shock absorber making pinning easier

Pinning with a hammer

Taping

Using strips of moistened paper tape (gum strip), tape up the back of the frame neatly to protect from dust and insects. Please do not use plastic pre-glued packing tapes - they are difficult to handle, do not look good and in the long term will leave a mess on the frame. Paper gum strip is easily removed by moistening if you need to open the frame. Leave taped frame to dry overnight.

Hangings

Fix hangings by pre-boring holes with bradawl and screwing in eyes then tying string or wire between the two. The hanging wire should be fixed at one third of the height of the frame - that is from the top and from the bottom. Tie the wire or string with care so it looks neat. Check that the fixings are stron g then your frame is ready to hung.

TWO
PROFESSIONAL /
SEMI PROFESSIONAL FRAMING

INTRODUCTION

My main reason for writing this section is that firstly, I am constantly being asked by friends all over the world as to how to set themselves up as picture framers and secondly, more importantly, I am constantly being told by fellow picture framers that they cannot make really good profits from their framing. I did, so what made me different? It took a while to discover because I naturally assumed every body makes the frames the way I do. When I discovered the difference, it was as they say, blindingly obvious. I "mass produce" my bespoke frames. In saying this I am not reducing the quality of the end product - or prostituting the noble art of picture framing. I am merely increasing my productivity, minimizing my costs and offering the customer a deal they rarely refuse!

So when you read this section, please understand my workshop and methods are all designed to fit this philosophy. If you frame one picture at a time, you can spend 20 to 30 minutes to several hours per frame. You will be pushed to produce 20 frames a week and to make a living each frame will have to be very expensive which in turn may loose you customers.

I have always found that people on average incomes have to work to budgets but the wealthier people also mind their expenses - that is how many are rich - and the seriously wealthy are few and far between and are pursued by large numbers of people after their money. You want to tap into the middle market, those vast numbers of people who live in the suburbs. To do this your price has to be right, along with your quality which has to be perfect and consistent. It is with this attitude that I went into picture framing. I had learnt the craft from experts but I wanted to make money so

I set out to produce as many frames as possible per week with the minimum of effort and strain on my part and as much money as possible in return, for no matter how satisfying the making of the picture frame is, the "paying-in" book at the bank is the real pleasure.

To achieve this high return, I decided that my frames should take a matter of approximately 10 minutes each (this was the rate I decided I could manage without the quality suffering). Hence, my method of framing pictures is as follows:

Measure up and produce a job sheet for all the pictures to be framed in the week. Cut all the frames together and then make the frames, cut all the mounts together, the same applying to glass, backing, assembly and finishing.

My framing week comprises of:

Monday
Measure up and write up the week's job sheet. Cut all the mouldings to size and make the first "L" of the frame or all the frame depending on your fixing system.

Tuesday
Finish making the frames then cut all the mounts (Mats).

Wednesday
Cut all the glass and backing. This will see all the picture frame components ready. Clean all the glass and leave the frames stacked overnight so the glass can dry.

Thursday
Prepare the pictures, fix them in their mounts, stretch tapestries, trim then work through the final assembly. When they are all stacked and pinned, cut the backing tape and tape up the rears, leaving them to dry overnight.

Friday

Make good any production marks on the moulding spines, fit/fix the hanging furniture, wrap the frames and invoice. Delivery to the shops Friday afternoon or Saturday morning.

By working like this, I felt I could control quality far better for by breaking the job sheet down into component parts, i.e. cutting all the moulding at once, or the mounts or glass, you can devote all your attention to that particular task, reducing the possibility of making a mistake on the machine or tool you are using. Constantly chopping and changing from one tool to another increases the chance of a lapse in concentration and therefore the possibility of making a mistake.

With this method I can produce u p to 150 bespoke frames per week but if I have a quiet week with say only 20 or so frames, the production is so rapid I can have a leisure week doing other things!

The other main benefit of this system is that it gives me room to manoeuvre on pricing - I work on the principle - quality work at a reasonable price. Applying the same, you will find that once you get known, you have tapped into a huge market.

As an exercise, just look round your walls, how many framed pictures are there? How many frames have you had made? Did you go back? Did the price take your breath away? Then take a walk around the streets at dusk, the time that lights go on but curtains are not yet drawn. You will be amazed at the blank walls - it's all potential market to sell picture frames.

As a proportion of the population, people who have large numbers of pictures on their walls are relatively few. There are many more who would like to have pictures frames but do not for often the simplest reasons - price and the fear of getting "stung". I have found it quite common that people are shy of choosing their frames. They do not want to appear ignorant, tasteless or vulgar. It's up to you to make them feel at ease and in control. If you do, your reward will be a long term customer who always comes back. The final choice is up to you but remember if you are in business, the idea is to make money. Look at the car industry. They mass produce both ordinary cars and luxury cars but both are still produced on a production line, one after the other!

For those who would argue that I have taken the "soul" and "pleasure" out of framing, try enjoying life when your business is not paying the bills! There is a common belief often put out by framers that you have to be 'arty'. Okay, be arty if you think it helps the image with your customers but the real secret of a good framer is giving the customer the frame he wants. What you might think is good taste might well be seen by another as hideous. So rather than 'arty', think customer's needs and taste - remember they are paying the money and are the ones who will have to live with your creation! It is also worth remembering that a satisfied customer will come back with more framing whilst the dissatisfied will take their business elsewhere!

SETTING UP

WHY PICTURE FRAMING?

You obviously have an interest in picture framing, so now its time to decide what type of picture framing you want to do.

a) Framing as a hobby for your own pictures but not on a commercial basis.

b) Small scale picture framing in your spare time and for a small profit - often called Bespoke.

c) Commercial Framing - either 'bespoke'. - I.e. you frame for the customer on a personal level or 'trade', i.e. you make picture frames for shops and volume customers.

Bespoke framing is traditionally like bespoke tailoring - the frame is made to the individual customer's requirements. Trade to shops framing is bespoke framing using the shopkeeper, as your middle man, to take orders and deal with the customer, i.e. you supply the samples and he brings the orders in - but this must be on a weekly turn around basis to be viable!

Trade to Trade is the production of huge numbers of very low priced frames of the kind seen in superstores for cheap prints/photo frames etc. . This for the most part requires power tooling and factories but even so the same basic principles pertaining to bespoke frames also apply here..

At this stage one has to ask two very important questions. Firstly - Picture framing is a very "clean" trade. You are dealing with people's pictures which might have great monetary value - and certainly always sentimental value. They really do not want them spoilt. So you have to be a clean worker, who is very self critical and has a keen eye for detail. Secondly - You are going to work with very sharp tools - guillotines, knives and cutters - all of which require razor sharp blades. They are dangerous and if you are careless or accident prone - be warned! This also applies to materials. The edges of 2mm picture glass are notoriously sharp, as are mount and card edges.

LOCATION OF WORKSHOP

If you are planning to frame for yourself, it doesn't really matter where you have a workshop - a dry garage will do perfectly well or a large garden shed provided it is not damp and has a strong floor. I started in a 2.44m x 4.88m (8 foot by 16 foot) concrete prefab garden building which I lined and insulated. The design was critical - I had to keep the glass in a little wooden summer house and glass cutting became a bit of an ordeal when it snowed as I had to keep the doors open to cut glass! - but it got me going until I cou ld afford to extend the prefab to 8.55m x 2.44m (28 feet by 8 feet). I still successful ly produced over a hundred frames a week in the original workshop!

If you have got the space, start at home until you establish yourself, then you can move to a shop or industrial unit. Wherever it is it needs to be in a place where customers can park, load their frames and bring in pictures without getting them wet. On more than one occasion I have witnessed a customer bringing an expensive piece of artwork for framing, unprotected, in a deluge of rain! Remember: art and picture framing do not like damp.

My personal experience of an ideal workshop is a space of approximately 9.15m x 2.75m (30 foot by 9 foot) - length is handy as the framing can be run like a production line, minimising the risk of knocking, gouging or breaking frames. If you have not got a single large space, have you got a bedroom or other room where you can divide the work? When considering your workshop, bear in mind hazards to customers - steps, slopes, slippery surfaces, unguarded equipment. If someone has an accident you could be liable and in this blame culture world we live in, it could be very nasty and very expensive. Whatever you do, make sure you have a very good Public Liability insurance cover. Do not just trust that your household insurance will cover you.

Finally and probably most importantly, remember that you need to be accessible to your customers to achieve a decent size potential customer base. A picture framing workshop on a beautiful, idyllic and peaceful Welsh mountain probably will not make you much money!

So in brief, your workshop needs to be:

1. Convenient for work and trade
2. Adequately large to be practical and safe
3. Have a dry and even temperature
4. Be accessible.

The other big consideration is noise levels. Power tools can greatly antagonise neighbours who in turn can bring the Environmental Health and Planning Authorities down on you and they can be very awkward. I had the experience once of finding the perfect location for my business to expand to, a large shop but the local Planning Department had other ideas as their response to my application for "change of use" was - you make picture frames, therefore the making indicates manufacture, therefore you must have an industrial unit, not a high street shop.

Also beware the dreaded Health and Safety Inspector when creating potentially harmful dust. It is interesting to note that the Health and Safety Inspectorate have the power to make your life very miserable, even if you work alone and do not employ anyone. I recently had a visit from a Health & Safety Inspector whose missionary zeal was to protect me from myself!

DESIGN OF WORKSHOP

To produce frames successfully with minimum damage to yourself, the frames and other people's works of art and for sheer working comfort, your workshop should be very carefully designed and made so as to allow modifications as your business grows and progresses. As mentioned earlier, I cannot stress strongly enough that it must have a dry even atmosphere. Warped mouldings and mouldy mount board are expensive write-offs!

I always run a dehumidifier and when closing up at night, regularly spray with insecticide (i.e., common fly spray stocked in supermarkets) to control pests such as the dreaded wood worm! Rats and mice can also be a problem so make sure they can not get in!

Storage in your workshop will require space for:

1. Moulding
2. Mount board
3. Backing board
4. Glass
5. Hardware
6. Sundries
7. Frames in production
8. Storing customer's artwork
9. Storing finished work.

Work in your workshop will require areas for:

1. Cutting moulding
2. Assembling frames
3. Cutting mount board, backing board and mount cutting
4. Glass cutting

5. Assembling and finishing.

Storage Space for Material

1. Moulding
Moulding comes in 3 and 2 metre lengths and stores very well high in the workshop - on cross bars near the ceiling or on wall brackets. You will also need to accommodate off cuts of moulding - plywood bins near the guillotine work well.

2. Mount Board
Mount board stores very well in vertical racks underneath the mount cutting bench. Again you have to allow space for off cuts storage.

3. Backing Board
Backing board can be stored with the Mount board or under the glass cutting table as you will probably have more than one type of backing board.

4. Glass

Glass will need a vertical rack in a position of safety where neither you nor your customers can get injured and from where it can be easily lifted onto the cutting bench. Remember you will stock two varieties of glass - clear and non reflective.

5. Hardware

Namely pins, nails, wedges, staples, strut back assemblies, mirror plates and a myriad of useful accessories. These should be arranged in boxes or in containers on shelves near the workstation where they will be used.

6. Sundries

Kraft paper, tapes, glues, fillers, stains, all store on racks or shelves to be readily to hand.

7. Frames in Production

As you make the frames, they will have to be stacked or stored in such a way as to avoid damage in the production process.

8. Storing customers artwork

This is extremely important - you require a secure cupboard, drawer or container where works for framing can be stored as safely as they can possibly be. Getting insurance cover on them is a good idea but I found it very expensive and some of the companies demanded Fort Knox style storage facilities!

9. Storing finished work

You need readily accessible storage where customers framed work can be stored safely - and removed safely. There is nothing worse than making a perfect frame for a customer and then damaging it as you give it to them!

Workspace in your Workshop

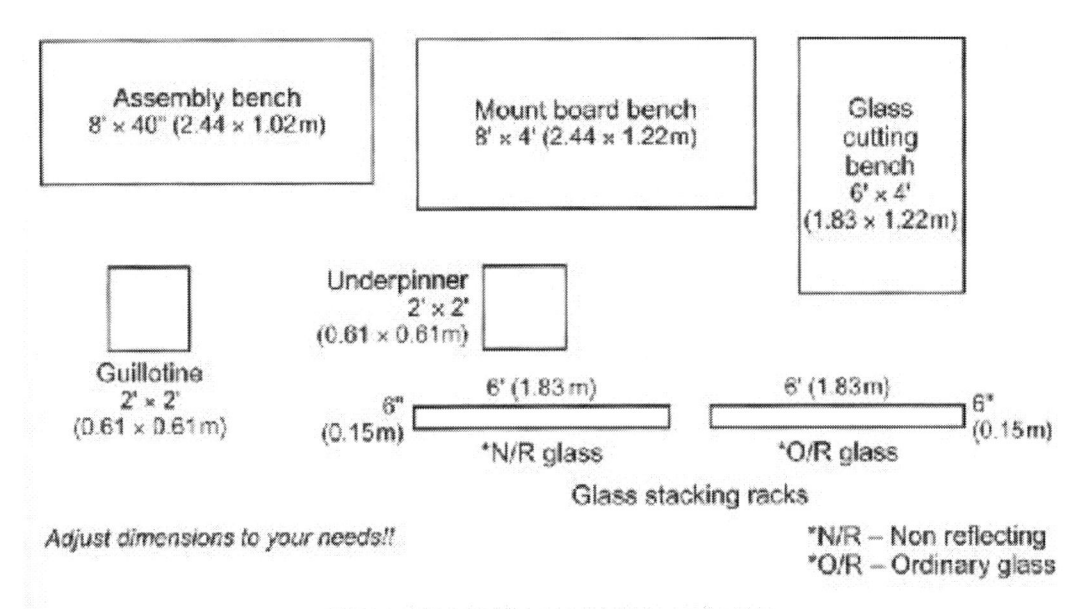

```
┌─────────────────────┐  ┌──────────────────────────┐  ┌──────────────┐
│   Assembly bench    │  │    Mount board bench     │  │    Glass     │
│ 8' × 40" (2.44 × 1.02m) │ 8' × 4' (2.44 × 1.22m)  │  │   cutting    │
└─────────────────────┘  └──────────────────────────┘  │    bench     │
                                                       │   6' × 4'    │
                                                       │(1.83 × 1.22m)│
                                                       └──────────────┘
```

Underpinner
2' × 2'
(0.61 × 0.61m)

Guillotine
2' × 2'
(0.61 × 0.61m)

6" (0.15m)   6' (1.83m)   6' (1.83m)   6" (0.15m)
*N/R glass   *O/R glass

Glass stacking racks

*N/R – Non reflecting
*O/R – Ordinary glass

Adjust dimensions to your needs!!

The main card cutouts to plan workshop.

1. Cutting moulding

Guillotines are usually a heavy floor standing foot operated double bladed mitre cutter that requires a clear run of 3 metres to its left for the moulding length and anything up to 3 metres on its right for the cut pieces of moulding. I have only made frames requiring lengths of more than 2 metres on a couple of occasions and it was easier to move the guillotine to accommodate the extra length.

2. Assembling Frames

Assembling the frames is done either on a framers vice or more commonly with an under-pinner which can be either free standing or bench mounted.

3. Cutting mount board etc.

For cutting mount board and backing board, I have always used a bench dedicated for the purpose with a mount cutting machine at one end and a card cutting guillotine at the other with card and board storage underneath.

4. Glass cutting

Once again I have always used a dedicated bench for glass cutting, a bench that is lower than the other benches and more robustly built with a "soft top" to protect the glass.

5. Assembling and Finishing

This is a most important long and spacious bench covered in soft protection to prevent scratching with space underneath for a powerful cylinder vacuum cleaner to ensure dust free assembly.

Dry mounting benches - Presses - are not dealt with here as I have not found them necessary in 25 years of framing. (But see Aspects of Framing - section viii - dry mounting)

REMEMBER: A CHAOTIC WORKSHOP DOES NOT INSPIRE CONFIDENCE IN CUSTOMERS

Before you start building your workshop it helps to draw a plan and pre plan the location of benches. The first requirement is to measure the rooms/spaces you are using and draw them to scale on a sheet of paper - graph paper is very useful for this.

1. Assembly bench - 2.44m x 1.83m (8ft x 3ft 3in.) - ideal but 1.83m x 1.02m (6ft x 3ft 3ins.) will do.

2. Mount cutting table - 2.44m x 1.22m (8ft x 3ft) - possibly with 20cm (8in.) extra for large mount/mat cutter.

3. Glass cutting table - 1.83m x 1.22m (6ft x 4ft), large enough to take sheet of glass.
4. Mitre guillotine - .60m x .60m (2ft x 2ft)
5. Free-standing under-pinner - .60m x .60m (2ft x 2ft)
6. Stack of glass along wall - 1.52m x 150cm (5ftx 6in.)

Once you have the outline of the workshop on paper, draw on a separate sheet - or a coloured card - the work spaces, i.e. the benches and tools in the plan (to the same scale) and cut them out. Now you can move the different benches around the proposed workshop to find the most suitable layout.

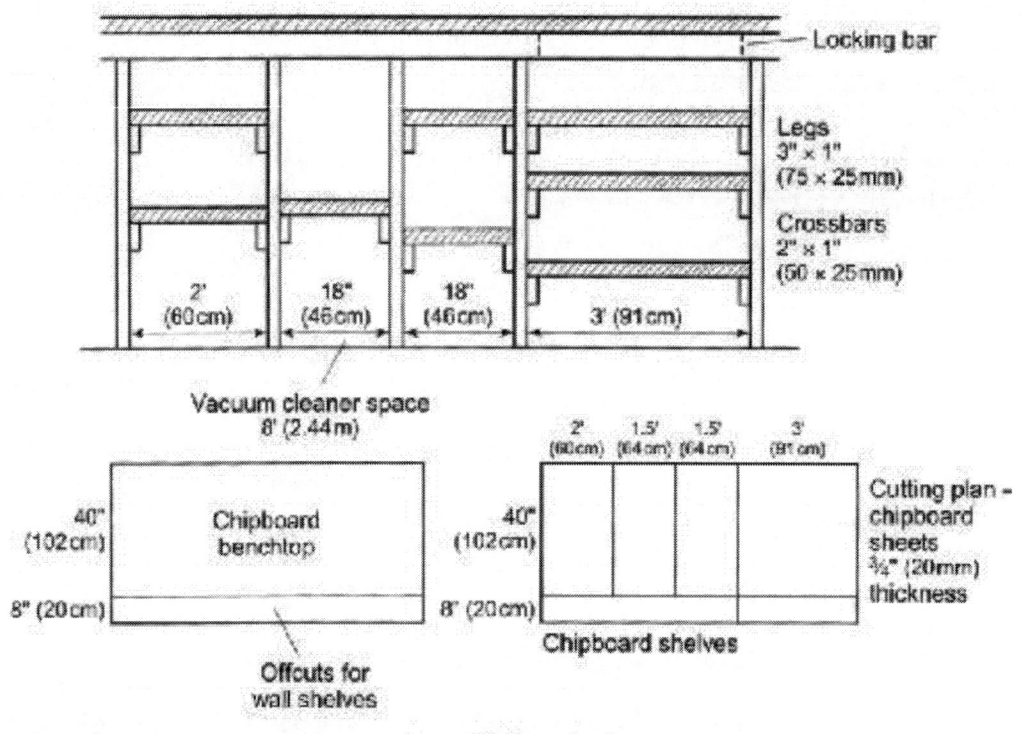

Assembly bench plan

1. The Assembly Bench

The assembly bench is the bench where you will probably spend the most time. Its size will depend on the (or what you expect your) largest frame to be. I always work on an outside measurement of .90m x 150m (3ft by 5ft). You will rarely have a frame more than .60m x .90m (2ft x 3ft) so the extra dimension gives you room to move. On this assumption, your minimum work area needs to be 1.02m x 1.83m (3ft 4ins x 6ft). Approximately 30cm (1ft) in from the left hand side of your bench (right if you are left handed) screw a 50mm x 25mm (2ft x 1ft) batten the full width of the bench, i.e. front to rear. This bar will act as a stop when you are firing or tapping fixing pins or darts into the moulding to close the back of the picture frame. The stop bar holds the frame while you apply pressure to the back.

The assembly bench needs as many shelves as possible underneath - all covered with padding so you can stack frames under construction, plus a space for a powerful cylinder/drum vacuum cleaner - the purpose of which I will explain under "Assembling".

The best paddings are the coarse dark grey blankets which you can get in surplus stores or any blanket that is not "fluffy". This is stretched and stapled over the bench to provide a non-scratch surface.

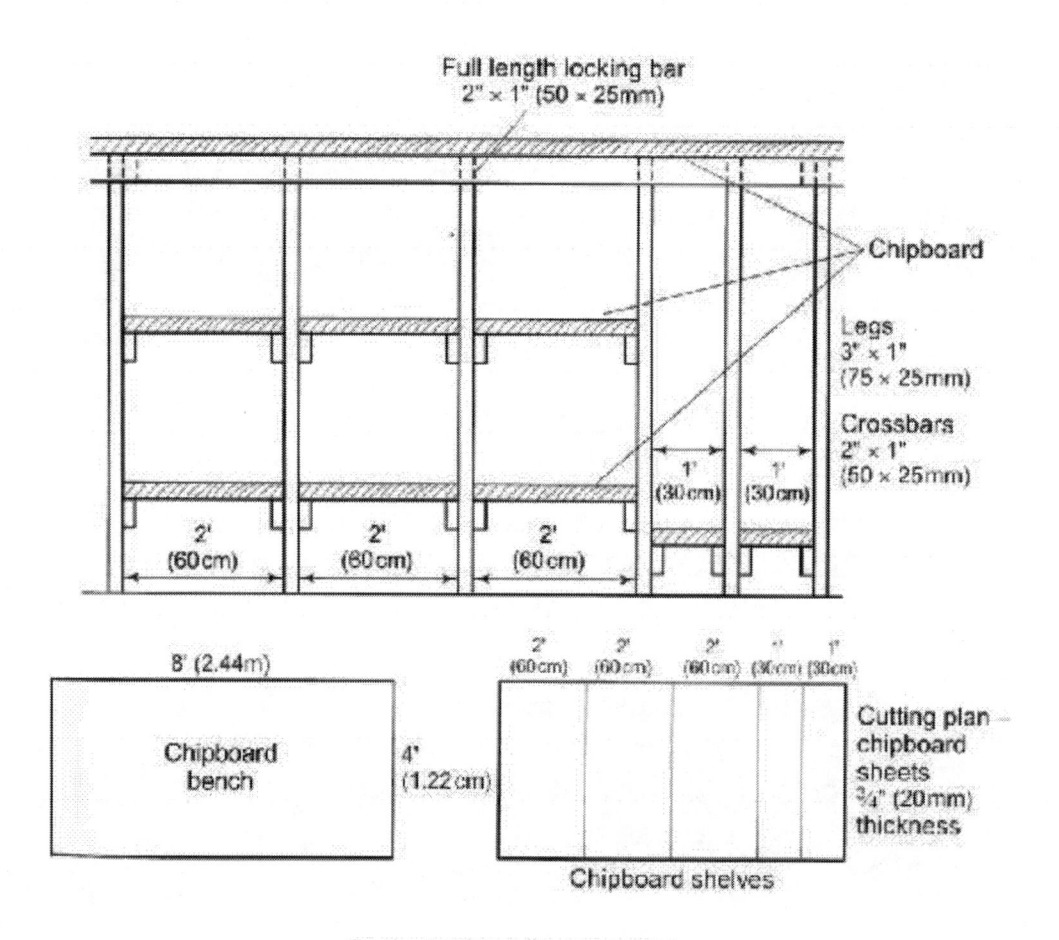

Mount cutting bench plan

2. The Mount Cutting Table

The size of this table will depend on what size of mount cutting machine you choose. I always choose the largest and best! You may, however, elect to use one of the hand mount cutters and if so, the necessity for this bench will cease. The best solution is to increase the size of your assembly bench. This also applies to the bench end guillotine for cutting backing board and mount board. A lot of framers prefer to use a steel straight edge and Stanley knife. The choice is yours.

Should you choose to go for the matt/mount cutting machine and bench end guillotine, then an 2.44m x 1.22m (8ftx 4ft) table utilizing a single sheet of 20mm (¾") chipboard will be ideal for 1120 x 815m (44.x 32in.) Double Imperial mount board.

3. Glass Cutting Table

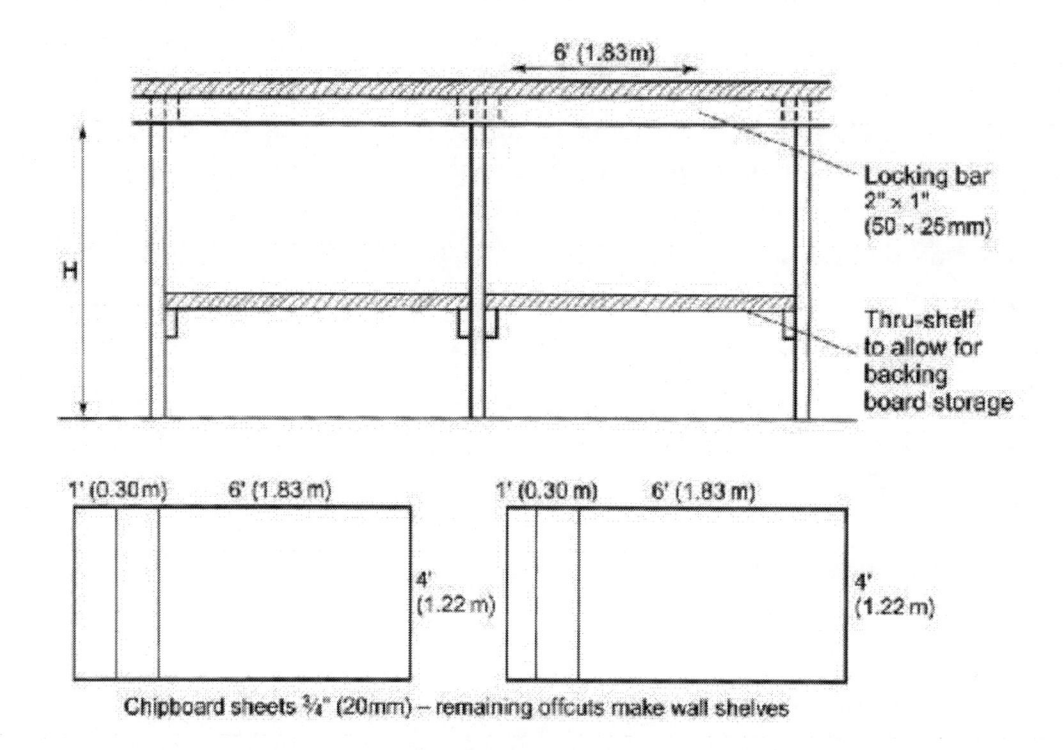

Glass-cutting bench plan

This must be a minimum of 1.83m x 1.22m (6ft x 4ft) to accommodate the glass sheets. It has to be firm/sturdy and have at least 2 shelves underneath for the flat storage of backing board. MDF or Hardboard are relatively heavy materials whose their weight when stacked on the shelves will give the glass cutting table stability.

To protect the glass, many people use a blanket but the ideal is 20mm (¾in.) insulating fibre board or "soft board", used shiny surface up. It is easy to change when it wears and a single slab on the table lasts many years. It is also very easy to keep clean of glass fragments which otherwise are liable to put scratches in your glass. You can also turn this table into a general workbench for the occasional screwing or rough work that you might have to carry out by simply lifting off the soft protection.

4. The Mitre Guillotine

There are both hand and foot operated models. I strongly suggest the free standing foot operated models. They are quick, efficient and a pleasure to use. Their actual base area is in the area of 60m x 60cm (2ft x 2ft) with support arms on two sides.

5. Free standing Under-pinner

A free standing under-pinner is on a base some .60m x .60m (2ft x 2ft), like the guillotine and is pedal operated. It can also be bench mounted or fixed to a wall. I like the free standing as it can be moved to accommodate awkward dimension frames.

6. Glass Stacking

The norm for buying glass is 25 sheets at a time of clear and maybe 10 sheets of non reflecting. For every sheet of non reflecting you use, you will probably use 50 sheets of clear. Non reflecting is not popular and tends to be used for photos or pictures where there is a light problem where the picture is to be hung. There is also the new UV Resistant glass to protect pictures.

Allow a wall space for the glass some 1.52m x 150cm (5ft by 6in.), placed so as to be easy to carry and lift onto the cutting table.

2mm glass is easily broken and very sharp, hence dangerous. Pre plan this activity with great care and ensure the glass stack is well away from public or occasional access.

Having decided on the size of the benches and machines you are going to install, make your card cut-outs and spend time arranging your workshop, then using a measure make sure you can work and move between the benches and machines easily and unobstructed.

Remember: you will be carrying frames and objects - do not cramp yourself!

Once you have designed your workshop and made the benches you will design the moulding storage and all the other necessary storage and hanging facilities around the benches and work areas for convenience of access.

CONSTRUCTING YOUR WORKSHOP

The following is the method I have used to set up 3 framing workshops over the last 25 years - all worked extremely well and all were reasonably inexpensive to produce. My last picture framing workshop I set up in 1998 cost £4,000 - that is with all the best equipment, timber and board to build the fixtures and fittings and a very good range of stock.

Benches

The first consideration when making your work benches is to work out the height of each bench. For assembly benches and mount cutting benches, stand upright and comfortably. Close your eyes and imagine yourself working on a frame, put your hands in front of you as if you were working - make sure you are comfortable. Measure the distance from immediately below your hands to the floor. This will give you the ideal bench top height. For example, I am 1.85m (6ft 1in.) tall and I work on benches with a top height of .99m (39in.).

Glass cutting is different as you need to lean over to run the cutter over the glass. For this stand comfortably and imagine cutting with your arms down - me asure the distance from below your hands to the floor. Once again as a guide, I have the working top of the bench 89cm (35in.) off the floor.

Spending hours working over a surface that is too low will play havoc with your back so as you are the main worker in the workshop, fit the benches for yourself. If necessary, should you take on someone to help out, you can always make adjustments.

Having decided on the position and height of the benches, the fun really starts when you make the benches!

For making the workshop that I have illustrated - that is 3 main work benches - you will require the following:
1. 20mm chipboard 2.5 x 1.2m (8x 4 ft) - 6 sheets
2. 75 x 25mm (3" x 1") whitewood PAR* - 44m (141ft)
3. 50 x 25mm (2" x 1") whitewood PAR* - 74m (242ft)

*PAR - planed all round

The above whitewood/pine is the minimum requirement for the benches, framing rack and shelving. To be safe, order an extra 15m (50ft) of each - it will always be used. The benches are made on the principle of a series of pine "ladders" onto which you fit the 20mm chipboard tops and shelving.

First of all, cut your 75 x 25mm (3 x 1in.) legs for the bench, using the height requir ement you calculated, minus the thickness of the chipboard top.

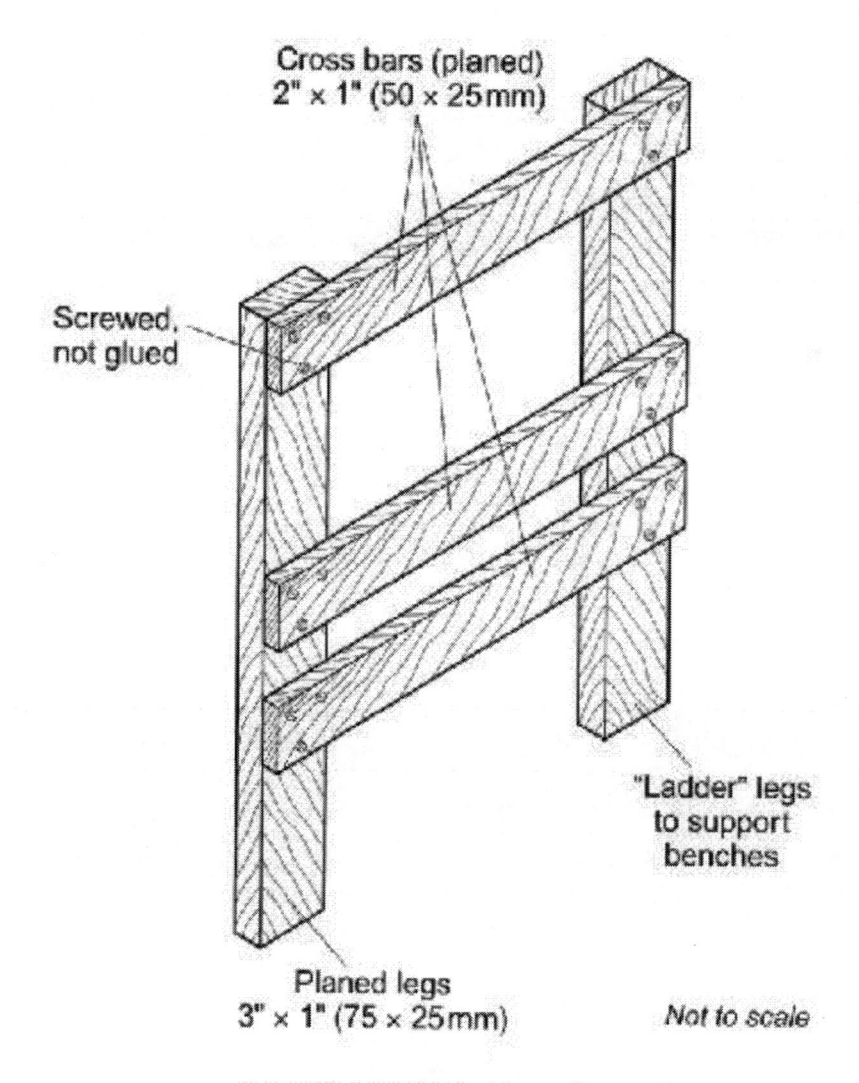

'Ladder' legs to support benches

Then using a right angle square, accurately screw on the 50 x 25mm (2 x 1in.) cross bars which have to be pre cut to the width of the bench, minus the two long 50 x 25mm (2 x 1in.) locking bars, that is 38mm (1.½in.).

Please note that when you buy planed timber, it is narrower than the size stated as the measurement is for sawn timber. Planning removes about

8mm (¼in.), so 50 x 25mm (2 x 1in.) planed is in reality, 45 x 20mm (1¾ x ¾in.). Allow for this in your calculations.

Each set of ladder cross bars will have to correspond to their opposite number to ensure you have level shelves. Once you have made the legs/ladders, fix the long locking bars to front and rear and offer up the bench to its final resting place. Check your levels and once satisfied, fix the bench structure to the wall.

Chipboard

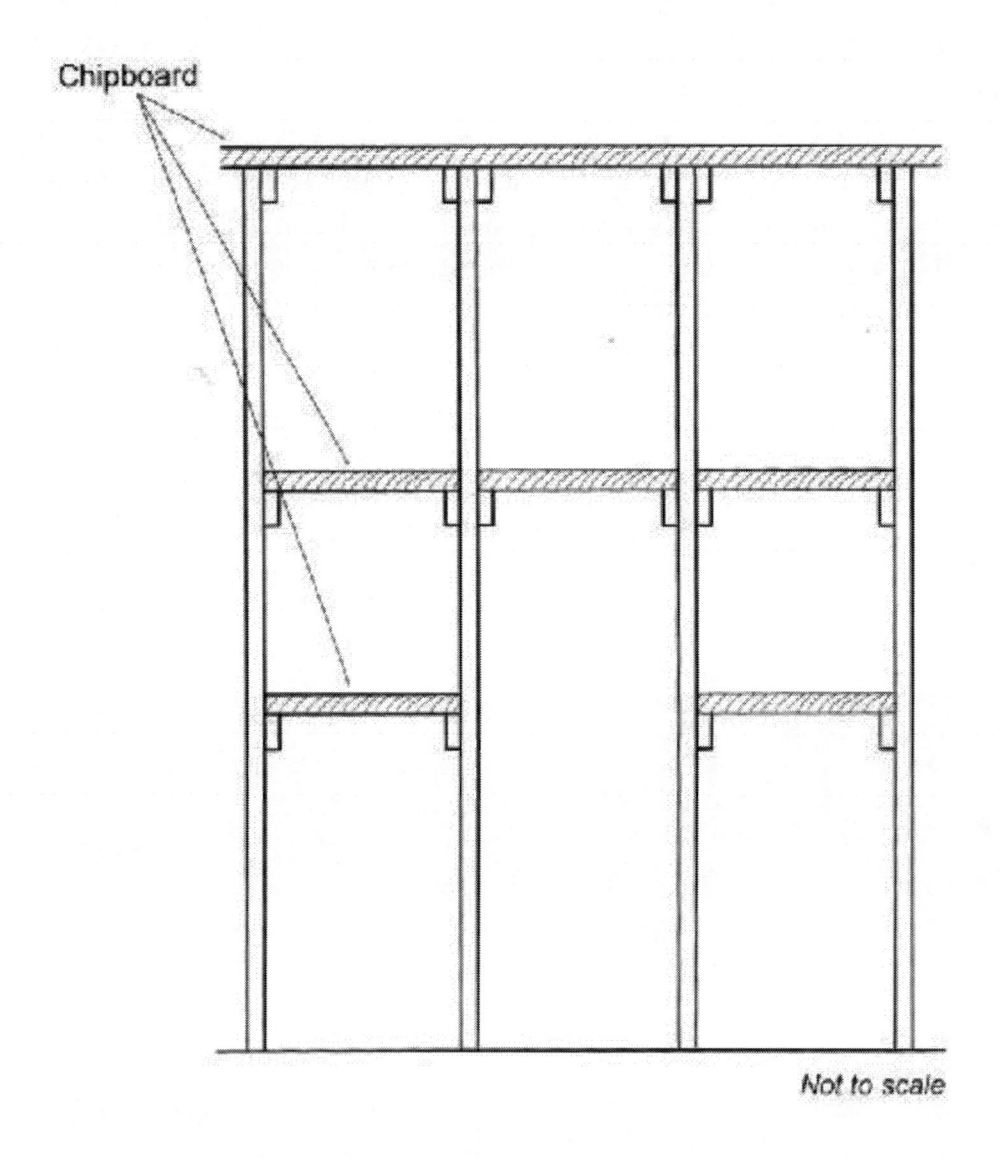

Not to scale

Cross bars on legs with chipboard shelving

Having fixed the structure to the wall cut and fit the chipboard and screw it down.

Always use screws as, inevitably, your requirements in the workshop will change and dismantling and reassembling the workbenches will be relatively easy.

Shelving

The off-cuts of chipboard should make 6 large shelves that can be fitted above the work benches. I recommend you fix them using the white or grey pressed steel shelving brackets that are readily available in supermarkets and DIY stores. A length of 50 x 25mm (2 x 1in.) screwed to the front edge of the shelf stiffens the shelf and makes a very good anchor point for clips and hooks to hang tools where they will be readily to hand.

These brackets also make ideal stacking systems for moulding. First, arrange three or four brackets on the wall to support the lengths of moulding - I work on three brackets for 2-metre lengths of moulding or four brackets for 3-metre lengths of moulding. Then screw a 30cm (12in.) off-cut of 50x 25mm (2 x 1in.) Batten to the bracket, stapling off-cuts of blanket around the wooden batten to cushion the moulding.

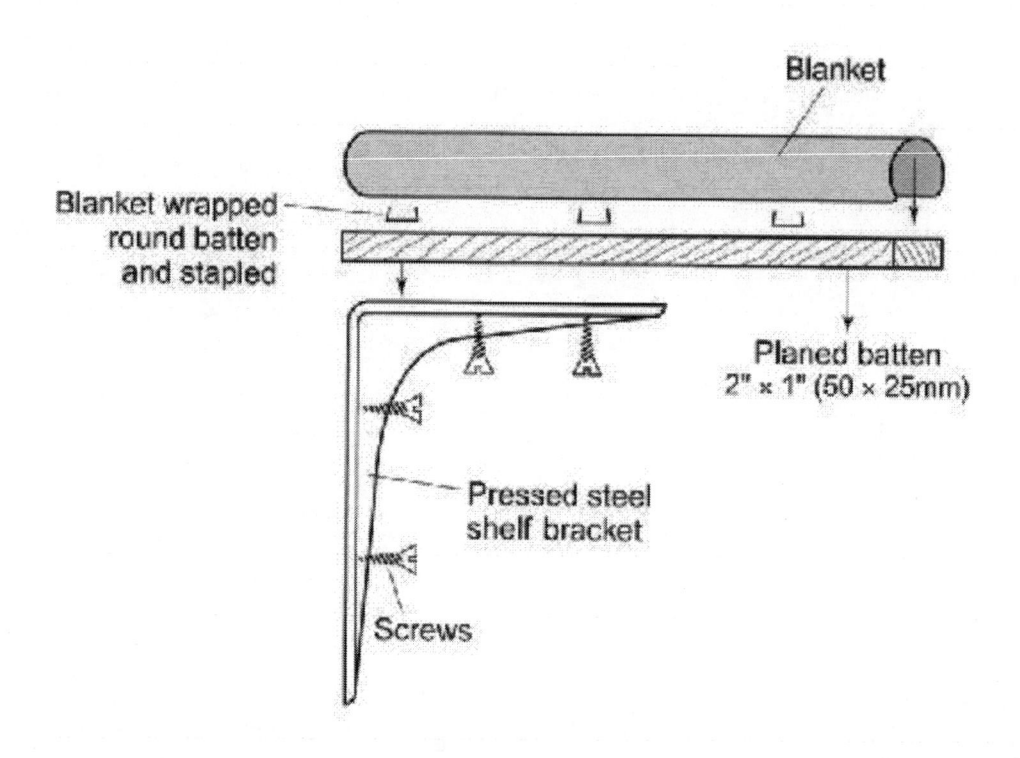

Blanketed moulding racking

Taking a shelf bracket, screw a 12, 14 or 16 inch length of 50 x 25mm (2 x 1in.) to the bracket, cover the wood in blanket off-cuts and fix these individual brackets on spare wall space - they are very useful for hanging frames that are not immediately required. You will find that you get pictures to re-do which are sometimes in a very attractive, perfectly good frame that the client does not want and you can always hang these away to be used later around another picture or to be restored. I used to make the picture frames for a large brewery. Their interior designers would say for instance that they were renovating a Victorian pub and wanted pictures to suit - many of those old discarded frames now hang in pubs round the country! However, be careful of old frames for the dreaded woodworm!

Lighting and workshop electrics

You require very good lighting for the workshop. I have always used the 1.22m (4ft) fluorescent (neon) tubes mounted above every bench to give excellent overhead light. I also have a .91m (3ft) tube mounted on the shelf over the assembly bench to boost the lighting when finishing frames or doing fine work.

I also have power points to the rear or side of all benches and power points on the front of the assembly bench.

Bear in mind that it is now illegal for amateurs to do anything more than minor electrical work themselves. You will certainly need to use a qualified electrician to fit out your work shop with the necessary lighting and power outlets.

The modern picture frame wholesalers tend to supply everything you could wish for and more, including all the fittings and ready made workbenches. My feeling is with regard to benches, build your own. It saves money and you have a custom made workspace exactly to your requirements, which is changeable to your ongoing requirements. The same applies to storage. Do you keep your screw eyes, mirror plates, pins and hardware in expensive purpose made stacking systems or as I have always done in labelled plastic food containers and old jam jars. My tapes hang on home made racks, the craft paper dispenser is 2 pressed steel brackets, two off-cuts of 75 x 25mm (3 x 1in.) and an old wooden curtain pole. The brackets cost me £1 and the dispenser has seen years of service and it still looks good! Ultimately the choice is yours - the size and style of workshop, be it all bought "gizmos" or a money saving but highly professional "DIY" workshop. You could say buying everything ready made saves time but to build the workshop I have described takes less than a week - and that at a leisurely pace. What is more, at the end standing back and looking at what you have built is extremely satisfying!

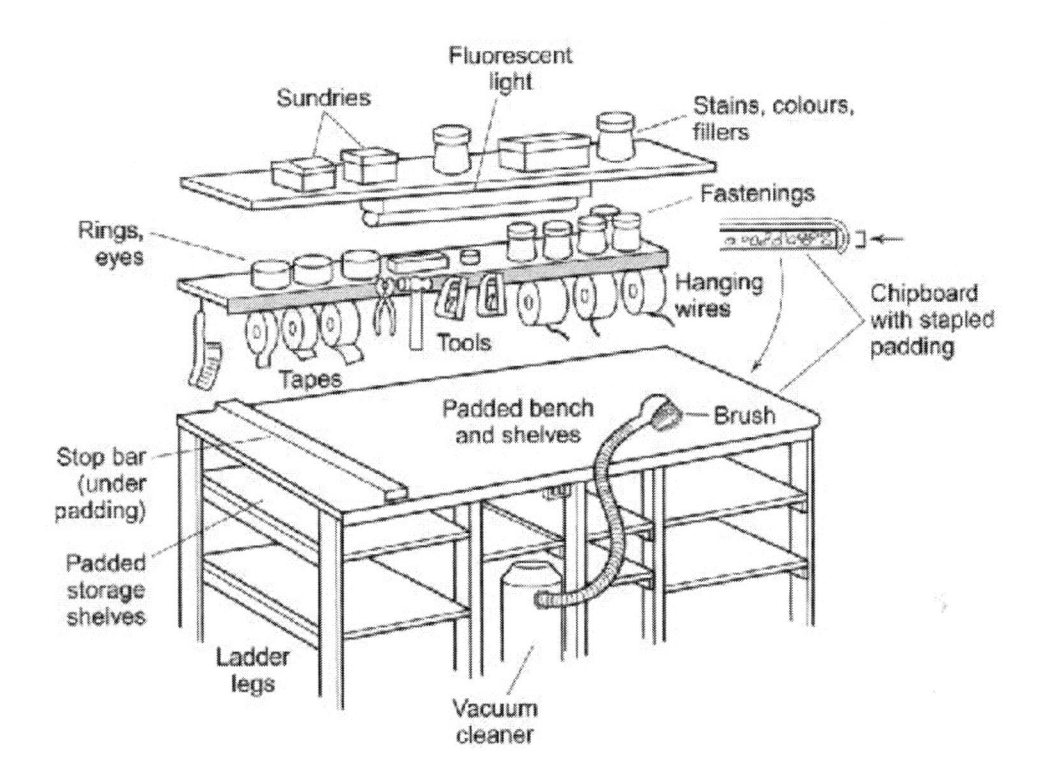

The assembly bench

EQUIPPING THE WORKSHOP & SETTING UP OF TOOLS

1. Mitre Guillotine

Having decided that you are going to buy the equipment you will need a machine to cut mouldings. Unless you are a small time hobby framer, don't even think of mitre boxes, saws and shooting block to plane your joints - a professional guillotine produces a join that is so fine as to be virtually invisible.

Guillotines all work on the same principle of a base or table top upon which the moulding rests. Adjustable, sliding rebate supports prevent the pressure of the blades crushing the unsupported rebate (or rabbit as the old time framers called it) which is the part of the frame the glass, picture and backing fit in A heavy triangular block slides through the base moved by a spring loaded foot pedal. Attached to the head is a pair of blades at right angles to one another and at 45 degrees to the base. The block also moves backwards and forwards so in essence your moulding is placed on the table, the rebate faces away towards the blades, the spine rests on the vertical shoulders at the front of the machine, the rebate supports slide under the "rabbit", the block is then moved away so the blade, moving up and down, takes a small wedge cut out of the moulding. It is then moved progressively in until the moulding is "nibbled" or cut through the final "click" of the blades makes a fine cut to give you a perfect double mitre.

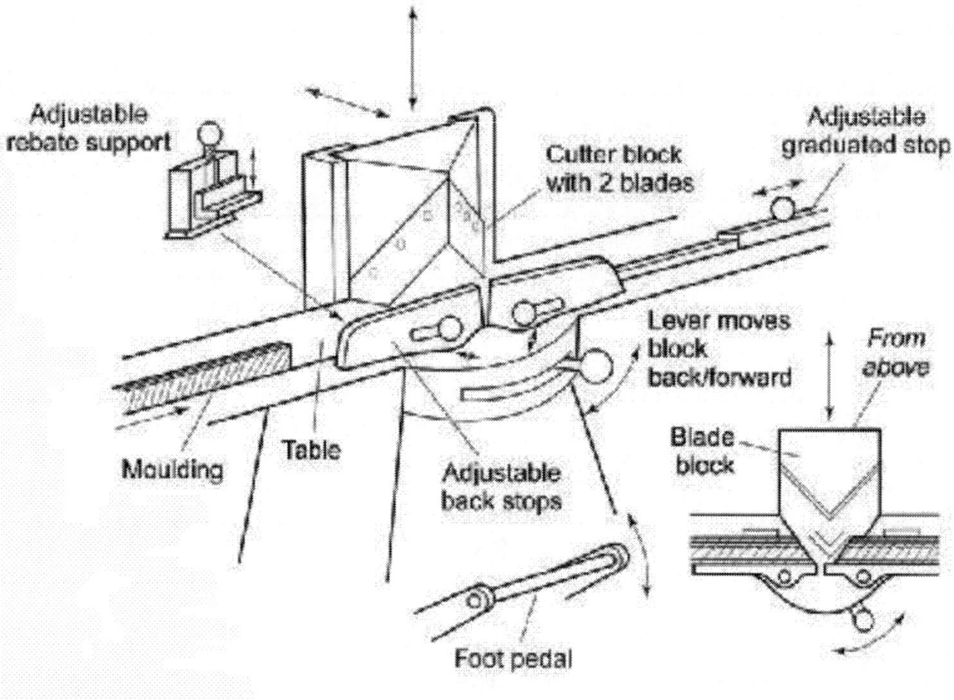
Adjustable rebate support
Cutter block with 2 blades
Adjustable graduated stop
Lever moves block back/forward
From above
Blade block
Moulding
Table
Adjustable back stops
Foot pedal

The guillotine will be supplied with comprehensive instructions. It is a simple machine and with a few hours practice you will soon be cutting perfect frames. The machines are calibrated to facilitate the measurement of the moulding you are cutting. Its various settings are also very precisely calibrated.

There are several very good makes of guillotine and apart from foot operated, there are hand operated bench models - okay for the occasional hobby framer but I would not recommend them for a professional - and of course the pneumatic models which are very expensive and which you could consider when you are making literally many hundreds of frames a week or if you are handicapped. Going pneumatic will hugely increase your setting up costs. You will need two other important items to go with your guillotine. The first is a very accurate "set square" to be able to check accuracy of machine and moulding cuts. The other is some form of collecting box for the moulding shavings which accumulate in volume and unrestrained can be a real nuisance underfoot. These collected shavings burn very nicely in a pot bellied stove - quite handy to heat the home or workshop!

2. Underpinner

In the order of making frames, your next requirement is joining the moulding pieces together. The current most popular form of fixing is an underpinner. This is basically a foot operated machine that the pieces of moulding to be joined are pushed into the holding bracket, then when foot pressure is applied, a padded press descends and hold the moulding fast whilst a "W" shaped steel wedge is forced into the base. Two of these are normally inserted a distance apart. They can also be stacked i.e., one pushed in after another forming a "pillar" of fixings through the thickness of the moulding.

Moulding

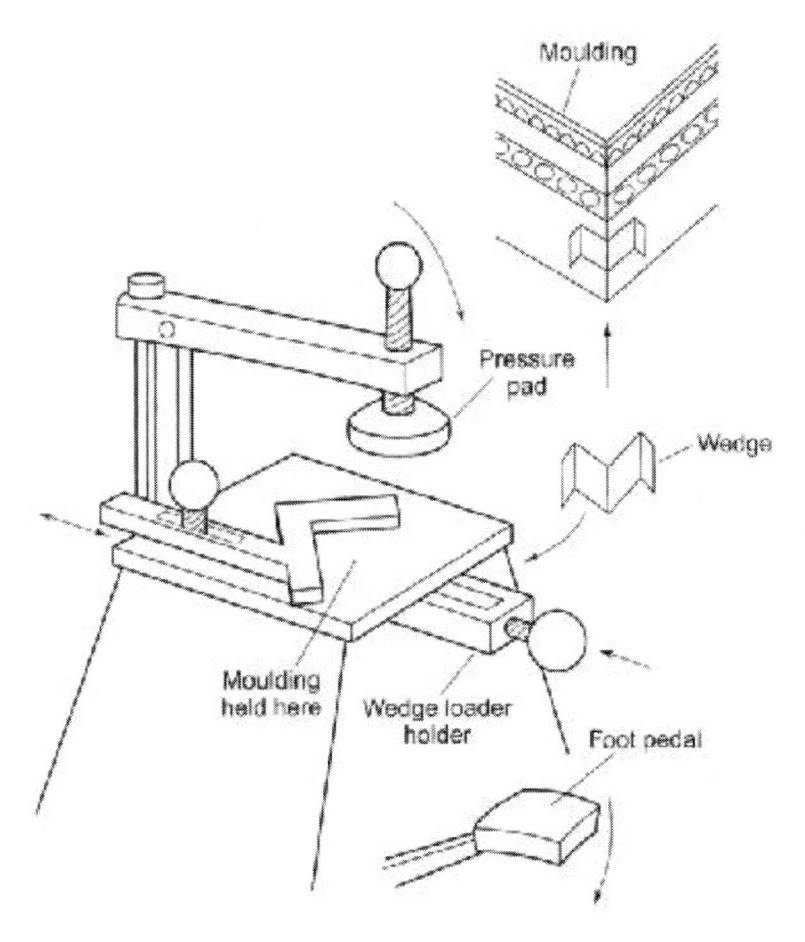

Pressure pad

Wedge

Moulding held here

Wedge loader holder

Foot pedal

Underpinner

The only drawback I have found with the underpinners I have used is the PVA white resin glue I use requires pressure to form a very strong joint. I don't feel the underpinner produces the required pressure so I have a clamping system I use to increase the strength of the joints. The beauty of the underpinner is the speed and the fixings mean that there is no making good on the spine of the moulding to cover pin or nail holes.

Once again there are hand operated underpinners or pneumatic and the same comments apply to this as to the guillotines.

3. Framer's Vices and Clamps

The traditional fixing method for moulding is the framers vice and pinning the joints in rotation.

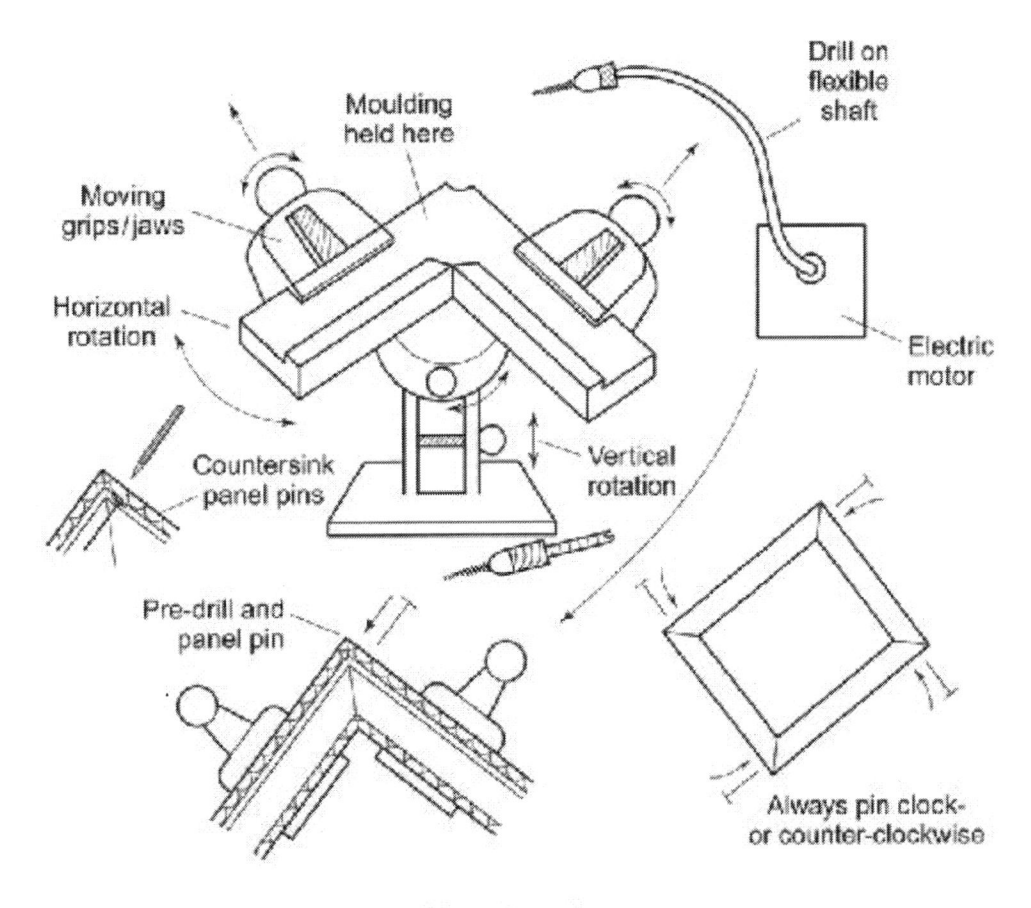

Picture framer's vice

The framer's vice is a traditional design with two clamps at right angles to take two sides of the frame with ample space to pin/glue the ends. The vice rotates 180 degrees and raises or lowers the angle of the frame through 90 degrees to get the best work position. I have always had one of these vices and consider it the best all round tool I possess.

With the vice I have a small electric motor that powers a flexible drill shaft holding a very fine bit to pre drill the moulding to stop the panel pins splitting the wood. There are numerous fixing methods, all based on clamps that pull tight round the frame requiring pinning after the frame has dried. I personally have two types of clamps that I have found efficient and cheap.

The first is the 'Stanley' string frame clamp - a nylon cord with plastic lock and four moulded 90 degree corners. These are put round the frame and tensioned then the joints adjusted to a perfect fit. To increase tension, I use a moulding off-cut to take up the extra cord and pull very hard. You can then underpin the frame so it is fixed and dried under pressure.

In the old days, framers used to get old bedsprings, cut them to form a "C" shape, sharpened the ends and used these to clamp the moulding while the glue dried. There is an Italian clamp system based on the same idea called "Ulmia Clamps". These are sharpened tensile steel springs of different sizes in a "C" shape which are applied to the spine of the moulding using special pliers. They do damage the spine but proper making good masks this and especially in the case of large dimension mouldings makes life very much easier.

There is in fact a huge variety of clamping systems on the market with new designs coming on the market every year. The best advice I can offer on clamping is keep it simple.

4. Mount cutters

The next machine you require is a mount cutter. The mount is the coloured card with an opening for the picture. The edges of this opening are cut with a bevelled edge and the best way to do this is to get a purpose made machine. They work on the principle of a base board with graduated stops where you place the mount board face down. A long hinged arm is then lowered on which is a running rail with sliding block holding the blade which cuts through the mount board producing (with care and practice) a perfect mount. It will produce large amounts of mounts quickly, painlessly and accurately.

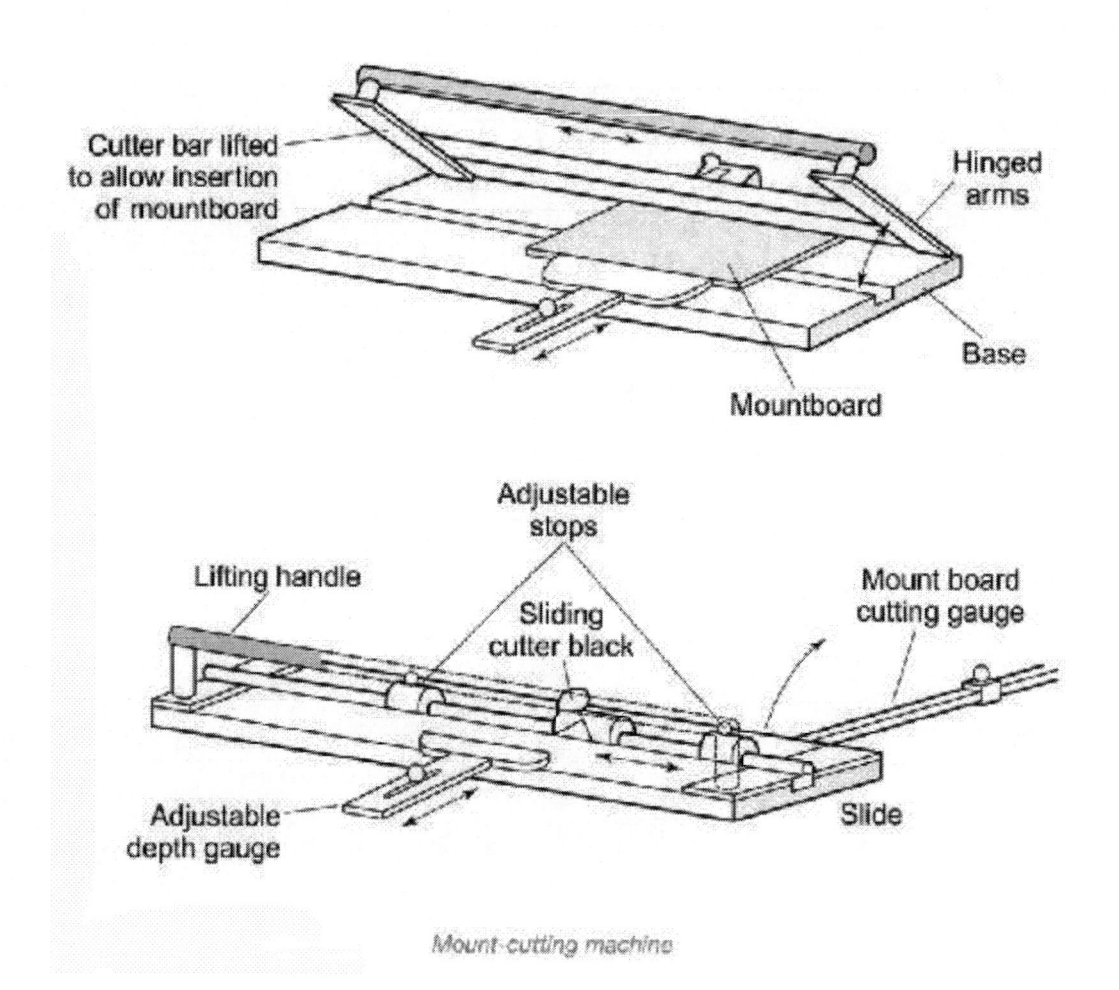

Mount-cutting machine

The alternative is mount cutting by hand. For this you will find various blocks and knives - I find them slow and tedious but okay for the hobby framer.

There are also oval mount cutting machines. These are very expensive and in my experience give very little return as after 25 years of framing, I still get very few oval orders! The main machines for oval cutting are either a micrometer mounted blade on an arm that describes an "oval" or a blade on a fixed arm that rests on a base that moves in an "oval", thereby cutting the board (or piece of glass which can be useful).

I would suggest leaving this one out. You can always buy one for fun at a future date to try and "loose" some of your awesome profits! I must admit I love my Teflon coated super deluxe American oval cutter but it doesn't make me any money. There is a simple hand held oval cutter that costs a fraction to the above machine which with practice produces perfect ovals. It is a plastic base with a metal arm holding the blade. You hold the plastic base down and the arm is p ushed round in an "oval" producing the bevelled moun t - it works for me!

5. The Card Guillotine

The card guillotine is the traditional 1.22m (4ft) long bench end guillotine, a long scimitar blade with a guard and self sharpening edge. They are wonderful for rapidly and accurately cutting backing board, mount board, trimming pictures - all round a most useful if expensive piece of equipment. Nevertheless I would strongly recommend one. The alternative is cutting using a craft knife and straight edge. Make sure it has a finger guard and in comparison to the bench end guillotine is slow, tedious and dangerous! The mount cutting machines normally have a built in method of cutting the mount board to size, usually an arm off the mount cutter with a vertical 'Stanley' type blade on the sliding block. This works well but still leaves you with how to cut your backing board.

6. Vertical Cutter

There are several makes of machine designed to cut vertically. These have cutter heads for card, board and glass and are designed for those with limited space. In essence they are a wall mounted frame, into which your material is placed and cut using a block running on a bar that is placed over the material.

I have never used one of these machines but those who do, swear by them.

If you are very short of space, one could help you considerably.

I would suggest in the case of this machine that you ask the suppliers for a demonstration. Try it for yourself before making the decision to buy. This in fact applies to any machine you decide to buy - get the supplier to demonstrate and have a go yourself.

There you have the main tools of your framing workshop, covering the greatest financial outlay of the business. My feeling has always been, have the very best tools, look after them and they will make money for you. They last for years and although expensive really do represent value for money. Some years back I completely re-equipped my workshop. I sold all the main tools off without any problem. They had all seen 20 years service and yet I sold them all to eager buyers for more than I paid for them new!

There is one other large piece of equipment I would not be without and that is an upright powerful cylinder or drum vacuum cleaner - the type the DIY stores sell with easily obtainable filters and spares. This is to clean the workshop but most importantly is set up under your assembly bench with the flexible tube, with a soft brush mounted on the end, to enable every frame to be vacuumed to prevent dust particles, hairs and splinters of glass getting left behind the glass. Using a vacuum thus, I have never had any problems. You would not believe the number of framers I have heard moaning about repeatedly undoing frames to remove flecks - so get a powerful vacuum cleaner!

There remain the various hand tools you will require:

1. Framing guns - dart guns and staplers. I use a standard stationery stapler with 6mm and 8mm. Staples. (Beware staplers for DIY as they are designed fo r fixing board, carpet and other heavy duty applicatio ns and will probably be too heavy/powerful for normal framing applications.)

2. For pinning the back of frames, I use a purpose designed framers gun that manually fires flexible darts into the moulding to close the back of the frame. (These also come in electric and pneumatic models.)

3. Several 'Stanley' type knives, all with fresh blades. Keep sharp blades to prevent damaging whatever it is you may have to cut. I use scalpels with throw away blades for fine work and these can be obtained from Art Shops.

4. Bradawl for boring start holes and an electric rechargeable screwdriver with socket attachments that grip screw eyes to turn them into the frame as well as screw on other fittings.

5. Pliers, blunt and pointed, plus wire clippers, several good pairs of scissors and canvas pliers.

6. Screwdrivers, flat and pozidrive/phillips.

7. A couple of hammers including a square framers hammer.

8. A good glass cutter for 2mm glass, set square, straight edge and plastic cutting Stanley knife blades.

9. There are various other tools and aids that are for specific jobs - none are expensive and I will describe them when I get to each stage of framing.

With the above, you should have a framing workshop that can tackle almost anything, but in saying this I am assuming that you already have basic DIY tools (power drill, jigsaw, etc.), which you might also need from time to time.

A word of warning: Whatever tool you are using, do not under any circumstances remove safety guards - I leave safety guards well alone and I still get perfect results. Don't listen to framers who tell you they don't need the safety guards. Not only is it illegal, it is highly dangerous. Always remember that making Picture Frames without fingers is well nigh impossible!

STOCKING THE WORKSHOP

Whe n st ocki ng yo ur wo rksh op, y ou wi ll fi nd yo ur su ppli ers lis ted i n the var io us d ire ct ori es i n you r loc al li brar y - which is a wonderful source of reference for whatever you want to do. The other source of information these days is of course the Internet. It often helps to have a supplier near you for emergencies. However, the distant suppliers have no problem dispatching goods to you and decent size orders usually come carriage paid (within the U.K).

Whilst stocking your workshop can now be done through one whol esaler, I personally prefer to keep accounts with several wholesalers to ensure I have, at the very least, back up supplies.

What you must remember is that with framing you buy the minimum stock you require and you only use it when you get orders. As the client base grows, you can increase your stock. Compare this to setting up as an artist where the artist has to produce the work, frame it, leave it in a gallery on sale or return, where the frame will undoubtedly get damaged - at the Artist's expense - and then if it is sold, you have the problem of

extracting the money from the gallery owner!

With framing, be it trade or bespoke, you have the framed pictures so, No pay, No frames. Bad debts have never been a problem as compared to the artist's world or any other business where you rely on the other people to stock and sell your products!

There follows a list of the various stock and materials you will need:

1. Moulding

As already mentioned picture frame moulding comes in 2 or 3 metre lengths and is made in a mind boggling variety of patterns, colours and finishes. It is normally wood base with various finishes but there are all plastic mouldings and metal mouldings as well. The plastic handles much like wood, the metal, if pure alloy, requires special cutting, often using mitre saws.

I personally avoid plastic and metal although I do stock the metal covered moulding which is a wooden moulding with a soft alloy cover with various finishes from bright to matt, silver to gold. They play havoc with mitre blades so I always charge extra and spend a few moments crying into my beer before thinking of the profit puts a smile back on my face!

The moulding is supplied in 30 metre batches although most suppliers will happily supply 15 metre batches - and often less - but for the most part charge more! 15 metres is the ideal amount of each moulding to start with. The Suppliers also supply samples - 15cm (6in.) long pieces of the various mouldings they stock.

When starting, it is probably best to start with 10 or 12 of the most commonly used mouldings. It is a good idea to make up right angles to aid choice, i.e. two pieces of moulding 8" long fixed at the mitre - and persuade the supplier to let you have another dozen or so samples to make up a decent sample display.

Your mouldings start with the narrow 15mm (½in.) mouldings to great big expensive 100mm (4in.) Wide mouldings that you will rarely sell, so it is best to buy these as and when you need them. Your wholesaler has a representative that will prove very useful in deciding on your initial stock. Keep it simple to start with and get a nice sober range from the small simple black cushion moulding through light and dark wood to silver and gilt which in turn goes through bright to antique, plus some colour finished mouldings.

You can gradually increase your range to some 35 to 40 mouldings in stock and if you are trade framing for local shops, you must keep the range displayed in the sh ops in stock - you will not be popular if you have to constantly tell the shopkeeper (who in turn has to tell his customer) that the order cannot be fulfilled or it will be late. Messed around customers tend not to return! This of course applies to mount board as well.

Remember, when starting your business, not to overstock or overspend on moulding - you will soon get a feel for what sells and in what quantity.

It is best to store your moulding in racks along the wall behind the guillotine where it is out of the way and easily accessed, or on cross beams at ceiling height if there is headroom. Storing the moulding high up keeps it away from moist air at lower levels. Remember to pad the racking, and stack it carefully: it is prone to warping and can be expensive to lose.

2. Mount board/Mattboard

Mount board is now normally sold by the framing wholesaler and comes in a vast range of colour, textures and thicknesses. It is now usually neutral or acid free - to prevent your framing masterpiece from turning the enclosed cherished picture yellow! There is far more expensive museum quality mount board which, as the name implies, is for the preservation of artworks but I use the standard acid free, bleached virgin wood fibre that is lignin free (a board that is buffered with calcium carbonate).

The sheet size Double Imperial 1120 x 815mm (44 x 32in.) is the standard (buying the largest is the most economical). Once again, you need to start with a range of 15 to 20 different colours . Do not worry too much about the huge range of textured and patterned boards. A range of cream to white, pastel and dark shades will start you off. I have at times been given manufacturers sample blocks containing beautifully cut samples of all their range - once again useful for the customer who wants something different and is happy to wait till you get his special order in! In practice I find that I need relatively few board varieties and only a few patternedboards.

Your stacking system for the boards is under the mount cutting bench in the 30cm (1ft) wide sections. The board is packed in vertical, on edge and I keep the sections tight by inserting a sheet of plywood of the same size as the boards and locking it in place. I carry 10 sheets of every colour but t o start, some of the suppliers do multi-colour sheet packs of 5 or 10 sheets that can help get you started. Remember that a customer will often come in with a set of prints or pictures that require a set of mounts so keep enough in stock for half a dozen identical mounts, i.e. usually 5 sheets.

3. Backing Board

For many years, backing board was card "strawboard" then 2mm thick hardboard came into fashion and more recently MDF (medium density fibre board). Both hardboard and MDF are still available.

There are some health fears with these materials: framers cut them using power saws which create noxious dust, so remember to wear a mask if you are doing this. I find that both boards cut easily and cleanly on the bench end guillotine, thus avoiding the problem of dust. There is also grey pulp board of several thicknesses, worth stocking for all sorts of backing jobs and finally there is the new foamcore boards which are polystyrene foam between two smooth outer layers, usually paper. This is much more expensive than hardboard or MDF but has its advantages - it is very light, easily cut and can be used in a variety of ways to make box frames or shadow boxes (see Making Special Frames).

You will probably eventually need to stock all the different backing boards to have the variety to match various frames but hardboard/MDF is the backing I use in vast quantities, probably 10 times more than the others. Start with sufficient stock for 20 or so frames, that is 10 or so sheets of each.

4. Glass

Glass for the most part is not supplied by the moulding wholesalers. There are various firms scattered around the country who supply 'A' grade float to framers. It comes in 90cm x 150cm (3 x 5ft) sheets and you normally buy 25 sheets at a time. Do not go to your local glazier as he will charge you a fortune! Look up Glass Wholesalers in the trade directories at your local library.

The second variety of glass you should stock is non reflecting glass. These are larger sheets, normally 1.8m x 1.2m (6ft x 4ft) but the supplier always cuts these in half for me prior to delivery. I usually keep 10 sheets in stock and these days rarely use them!

The third variety of glazing is plastic glass. These are "styrene" glass clear plastic sheets, either clear or non glare, protected on both sides by a layer of polythene. They are UV stabilized and cutting is with a special blade which "scores" the plastic. You then snap it off over the edge of the bench. It has one great drawback in that it collects dust as it picks up a static electrical charge and will probably drive your mad! I only use it if specifically requested or if I am framing one of those long school or college photos that have been taken on a rotating camera - the sort of photo that is 1.2m x 15cm (4ft long and 6" wide) - the flexing would probably break 2mm glass. Fortunately these seem no longer fashionable as I have not had a long school photo to frame in years.

There is also a new UV protecting glass which is worth stocking for pictures that need special protection.

5. Sundries

This is the final heading for the major stock section and concerns those various fixing and fittings that are classed as frame furniture. As a rough guide you will have:

1. Pins, nails, staples and wedges and blades for your guns and cutters - supplied by the wholesaler who supplied the tools.

2. Picture hanging furniture, namely screw eyes, ring s, D-rings, mirror plates and several other "patent hangings", plus the picture string (non stretch or picture wire). I carry three thickness of the steel cored brass wire for hangings - I never use string. (I had an early accident - a very irate customer came back with a broken frame. She had hung it up, stood back to admire it and it had fallen with a seismic crash at her feet - the string had come adrift. I have avoided string ever since and never had a repeat of the very embarrassing incident.) You will then have turn buttons, strut backs and clip springs for supporting photo frames. There are numerous products to aid framers from canvas fixings to frameless glass clips, but if you start with a good pinning system, a hanging system and mirror plates and turn buttons, you c an add others as you grow. I also carry brass picture hooks and pins as I always give a free wall hanging with every frame –it's a nice touch and always appreciated.

3. Tapes. I use 4cm, 5cm & 7.5cm (1in., 2in. & 3in.) brown gummed paper tape for finishing the backs. (I will explain why under "Finishing Frames".) I keep my tapes on home made rollers under the shelf in front of the finishing table along with rolls of 2.5cm & 5cm (1in. & 2in.) masking tape, sellotape and brown vinyl tape on a gun dispenser for p arcelling up frames. Finally you will need a very good quality double sided tape for hanging pictures behind mounts. Make sure it will not damage the pictures. I use conservation quality tapes for this purpose.

4. Copydex is a useful glue to carry in the workshop and for gluing moulding I use Resin PVA wood glue - it is non toxic, safe and strong.

5. I also carry a 90cm roll of Kraft paper and a roll of bubble back to wrap and protect completed framing jobs. Remember that presentation is important : if you deliver your customer's expensive frame in old waste paper like second rate fish and chips, you probably won't see them again!

MAKING PICTURE FRAMES

CATEGORIES OF PICTURE FRAMES

You will find the frames you make will fall into basic categories which are:

1. Frames only
2. Frames with glazing
3. Frames with mounts (mats) and glazing
4. Frames for tapestries/embroideries

Occasionally you will get a frame that does not fit into these categories - coins, medals, 3 dimensional objects - and I will deal with these under their own heading in "Aspects of Framing".

1. Frames Only

This is the framing for oil paintings or acrylics that are either on a board or canvas and do not require glazing. You may also get notice boards, maps, diagrams, etc., to frame which the customer for one reason or another does not want glazed.

2. Frames with Glazing

These are objects or pictures to be framed behind glass. They are known as "Close Frames" and can include certificates, pictures, photographs, etc. Whenever you "close frame" a picture remember to leave a space between the end of the rebate and the paper to allow for expansion and contraction of the picture with changes in atmospheric conditions.

Expansion space

Backing

Glass

Moulding

Moulding

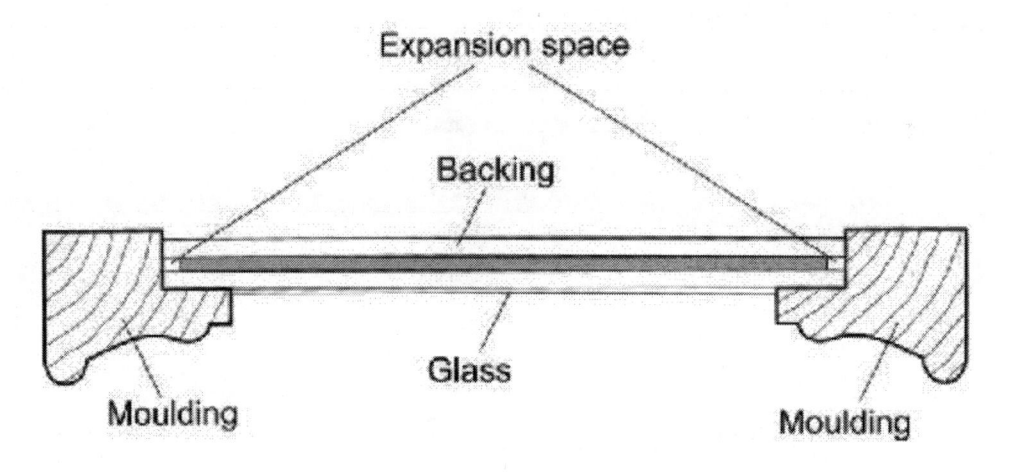

Allow for picture expansion

If a picture is "tightly" framed, when it expands with a change of atmosphere, it will "cockle". When you look at framed pictures you will often notice that the picture has wave like ripples over the surface. They look unsightly and are caused by framers "cramming" the picture into the frame so when it expands it "cockles". In fact once you have an interest in framing, you will find yourself constantly studying frames - in friend's homes, galleries, shops - it can become a bit of an obsession, a sort of "spot the cock up" and you will be amazed at the botched jobs you see! Don't whatever you do go round loudly pointing out the faults - you may find your circle of friends rapidly diminishing! The habit is, however, very good for your own quality control.

3. Frames with Mounts (Matts)

A mount, or a mat as it is called in the USA, is a coloured sometimes textured card surround that is placed behind the glass and before the picture. It has an aperture cut out to reveal the picture and the aperture itself is cut with a 45 degree bevelled cut to reveal a pleasing white border between mount and picture.

The picture is hung behind the mount with a fixing along its top edge - the other three edges of the picture remain free to allow the picture to expand and contract naturally. The other good reason for a mount, apart from the aesthetic appeal of enhancing the picture, is to keep the picture off the glass. Glass is very susceptible to temperature change so a space protects the picture.

4. Frames for Tapestries, Embroideries and Cross-stitches

The fourth category of frames you will make a lot of, are the tapestries, embroideries and cross stitches that many framers refuse to do. This is a very lucrative special service you can offer. The artwork is "stretched" either over a frame or a board and fixed in place, usually sewn - I abhor glue in such circumstances. Recently I was brought in an exquisite piece of work - a cockerel embroidered onto a panel. The artist or creator had spent many hours quite literally embroidering in every feather. The effect was absolutely stunning. You can imagine my horror to discover that the previous framer (an alleged professional - I've still got his label and address on the workshop wall, I stick pins in it from time to time!) had glued the moun t to the front of the artwork and glued the artwork itself to the backing board. The only thing I could do was to spend an entire day carefully unpicking the piece and cleaning off the glue. It framed up a treat, stitched onto a piece of museum board and framed. Under the circumstances - and I think you will agree - I did not charge the customer the full cost of my time but I strongly suggest you avoid glue!

MAKING THE FRAMES

1. Job Sheet

You will require a job sheet for making your frames. I always use an off-cut of mount board and onto this I write all the measurements and calculations: Moulding number and type, mount board number and colour, type of glass, type of picture (the pictures are kept in their secure store until they are ready for assembly into the frame). The idea is to minimise the chance of mistakes and accident. Make it a rule to do this if you have one or 100 pictures to frame. Also use the same sequence on the job sheet so you do not transpose dimensions. Keep the dated job sheets in a box so you can always refer back from order to job sheet to invoice.

Order No.	Picture	Picture Size	Mountboard Colour	Mountboard Width	Frame size/ Backing	Glass	Notes
123	OIL ON CANVAS	20" x 30"			20 x 30		FRAME ONLY
224	PHOTO	10" x 8"	BLACK	2"	14" x 12"	O/R	
225	W/COLOUR	16 x 12	CREAM	3"	22 x 18	O/R	GREEN WASHLINE

Job sheet

You should always endeavour to keep your customer's pictures secure and limit your handling of them. By this I mean when writing up your Job Sheet, measure and note down all relevant details of the picture at that time then put it way in a secure place only to be returned for insertion into the finished frame. DO NOT keep customer's property "floating" around the workshop - the risk of accidental damage is too great!

2. The Moulding

Take out the length of moulding, or mouldings to be cut, unwrap them carefully and closely examine the lengths for flaws on their faces, i.e. check for damage, warps or twists. If the length is bad I always keep it to one side, notifying the suppliers and showing the length to the representative when he calls.

Moulding is packed in individual lengths, multiples or pair at the factory and you will occasionally find when you unwrap them, lengths twist or bend. It happens and it's Murphy's law that you will always have a problem with the last length and an impatient customer.

When moulding is manufactured, the wood is first milled to the required profile. This is done with two lengths simultaneously. They are joined like Siamese twins along the rebate and are subsequently split before the final finish is applied - the ornate or decorated frames with a "compo" layer which can also be called "gesso", originally gypsum or chalk or plaster of Paris but more recently a plastic mixture, which is applied to the face of the wood. A metal roller with the pattern cut into the surface is then passed over the gesso, imprinting the pattern on the frame. This is usually applied to left and right mouldings before they are split. What is very important to remember is that the left and right hand will not marry up, therefore your moulding must be of the same batch and same side to get a perfect frame. Off-cuts or remnants that do not match are best kept in your off-cut box for a smaller frame that will utilize the off-cuts. Do not try and make frames with lengths from different batches. They will not work.

Having checked your moulding, you can cut the individual pieces on the guillotine. This is a simple operation that entails setting the stop measurement, trimming the end of the moulding, sliding it to the stop, setting the rebate supports and using multiple cuts to "nibble" through the moulding to achieve two perfect mitres. Remove the cut piece, slide the length on and cut another piece. Now move the stop to the second measurement and repeat the process for the final two lengths. In cutting, it is important not to have any damage to the face of the moulding either on the length or at the cut. Never make a frame then try to make good a bad mitre. Your guillotine is a precision tool that properly set up will give you a mitre joint that is so fine as to be virtually invisible. Anything less than perfect, re-cut the frame. The reject pieces can have the flaws and damage cut out and used on frames of different dimensions. Having cut the frame, check under the rebate. You may find some bits of wood splinter on the underside of the rebate. Trim them off to prevent them getting into the joint.

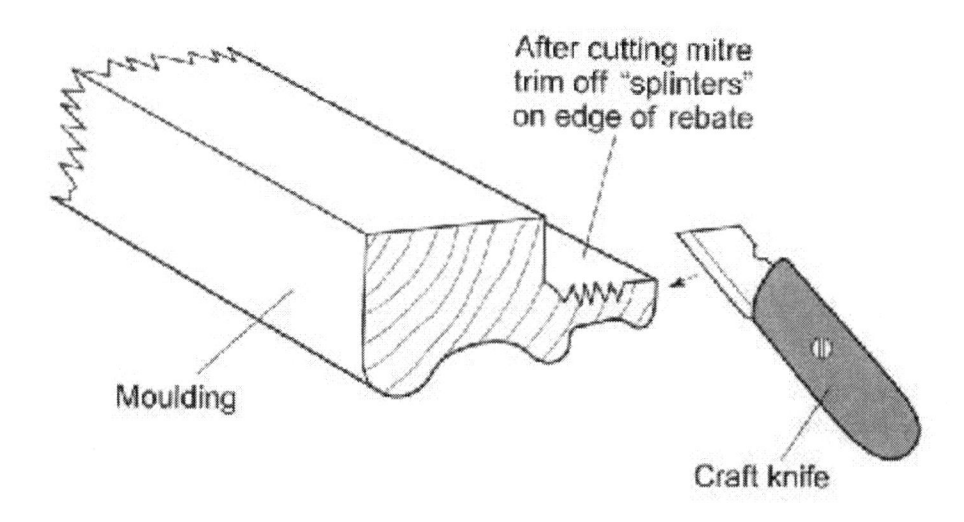

Trim splinters

When cutting the frame, it is essential that the moulding is absolutely flat on the moulding base so that the blade cuts an exact 90 degrees to the moulding. You require an exact 45 degree mitre to join the frame up and the mitres must go exactly face to face. If the moulding is not held flat you will find your frame does not lie flat.

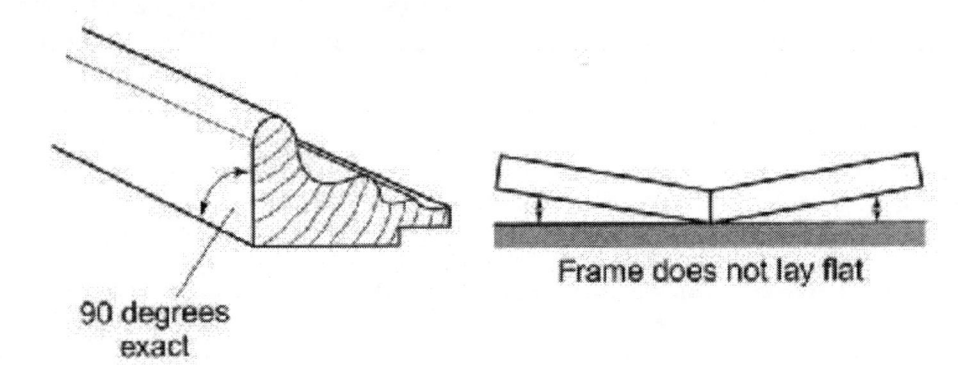

90 degrees exact

Frame does not lay flat

If the frame does not lie flat, your moulding was either warped or you did not have the moulding flat on the guillotine table.

3. Assembling Your Frame

Having cut your frame, it is time to assemble it. (see Hobby Framing for cutting by hand. Here my primary object is to produce "professional" quality frames and you will never get the required results using hand saws, mitre blocks and shooting blocks). The traditional and still often used method is clamping and pinning but the underpinner has become the main means of fixing over the last 20 years. I use both the underpinner and framer's vice and pins.

With a framer's vice, place a length and width into the vice and adjust them to make a perfect fit . Having done so, remove one piece and cover the mitre with a thin layer of glue and return it to the vice. Then pre drill a pair of holes and insert the panel pins. Tap them down and using a centre punch countersink them below the surface. Remove from the vice and set aside and repeat operation with the second pair of lengths or "L's". Always pin in the same direction and always put the length and one width on the same sides. This will ensure you get a frame whose halves (L's) marry up and are pinned in a clockwise or anticlockwise direction. Leave the "L's" overnight to enable the glue to dry completely. A good framers vice holds the two glued pieces of moulding together with sufficient pressure to ensure that you get a very strong mitre joint when pinned.

To underpin your frame, take the length and width of the moulding, place them on the table of the under- pinner, adjust the backstop to the position you want your wedge, adjust the pressure pad above to hold the moulding without crushing the face, glue and insert the wedge, or wedges if required. Once again I tend to make the "L's" and leave them to dry overnight before completing the frame.

As I said earlier, I am not convinced as to the strength of the glue joints using the under-pinner so with any frame larger than A4 size (as a rough guide), I tend to clamp the frame. For this purpose I normally use the 'Stanley' plastic picture clamps or the 'Ulmia Clamps' for larger moulding.

Having clamped the frame, I then set the under-pinner and "wedge" the joints.

You then have a complete frame, pinned (wedged), glued and clamped under pressure. Leave it overnight for the glue to dry. Remember that with white PVA resin glue, once dried under pressure, the joint will be stronger than the wood! In the latest under-pinners the pressure problem is dealt with by to othed claps that pull the moulding in so that the corner is automatically held and pinned under pressure. At all times, remember to protect the face of your moulding and do not allow glue to come through the joint to deface the moulding. I always keep cheap rolls of toilet paper scattered around the workshop for wiping away glue, etc.

MAKING FRAMES (PROFESSIONAL)

1. Guillotine trims off moulding length to obtain first mite cut.
Note rebate supports set under rebate on left hand side of moulding.

2. Guillotine trims (nibbles) through moulding in several cuts.

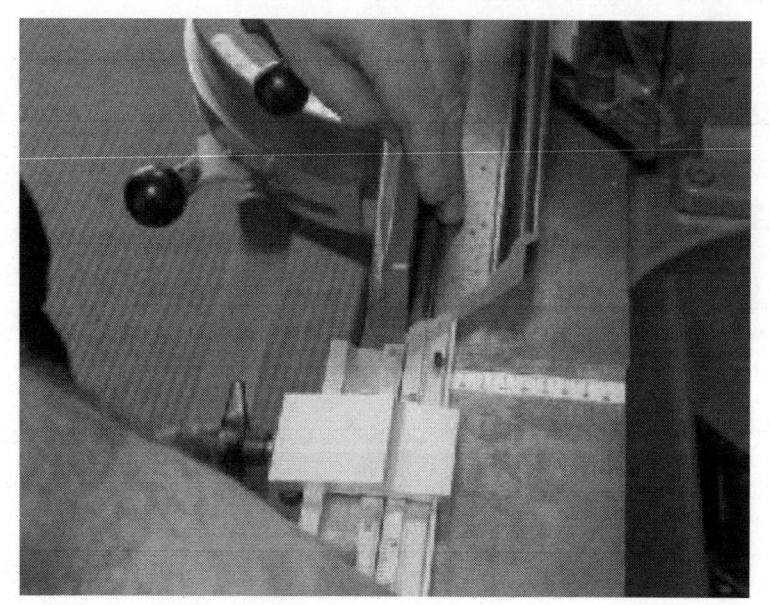

3. Set the calibrated scale for the length/width of frame.

4. Cut length to size.

5. Nibble cuts protect guillotine/moulding from excessive force.

6. Setting the underpinners top pressure pad which hold the moulding in place while pinning.
(Note: this underpinner is a pneumatic model.)

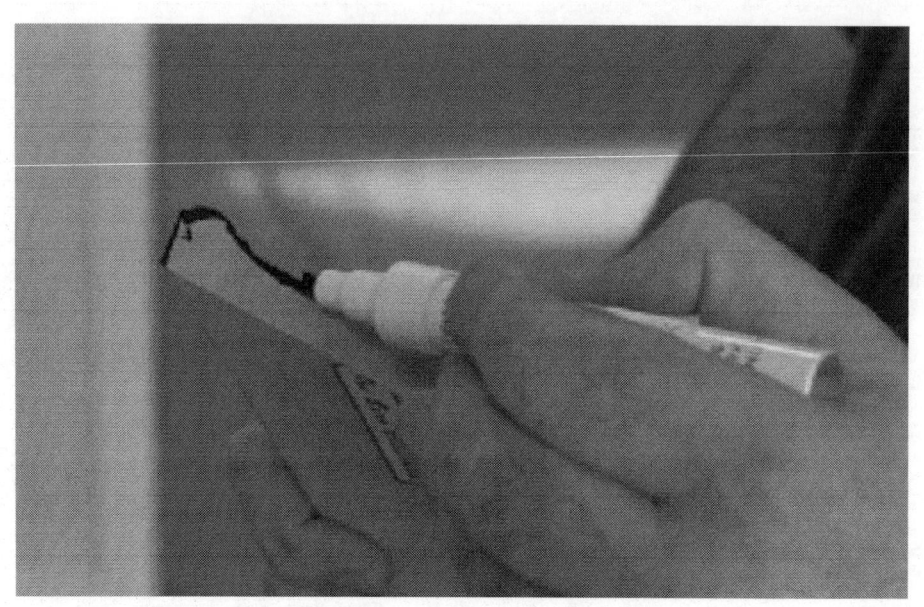

7. Mark top edge of mitre with indelible black felt pen to ensure that no light wood shows on the dark moulding face (useful tip!)

8. Hold moulding length in underpinner, lower pressure pad and insert wedge.

9. Shows the wedged and glued mitre - the process is repeated for all corners.

DETAILS OF FIXINGS - UNDERPINNER WEDGES

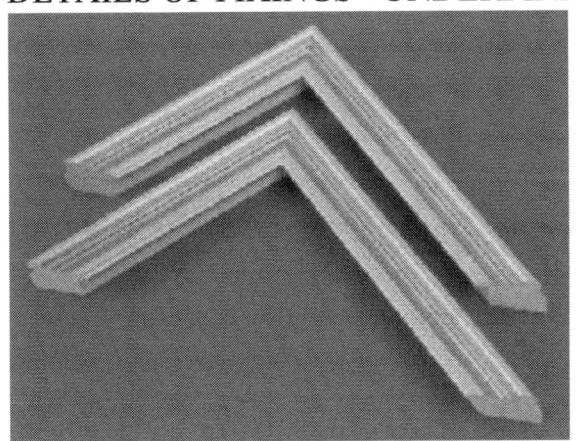

1. Shows 'L's of moulding pinned and glued - it is often better to leave these to dry overnight before making up the final two joints.

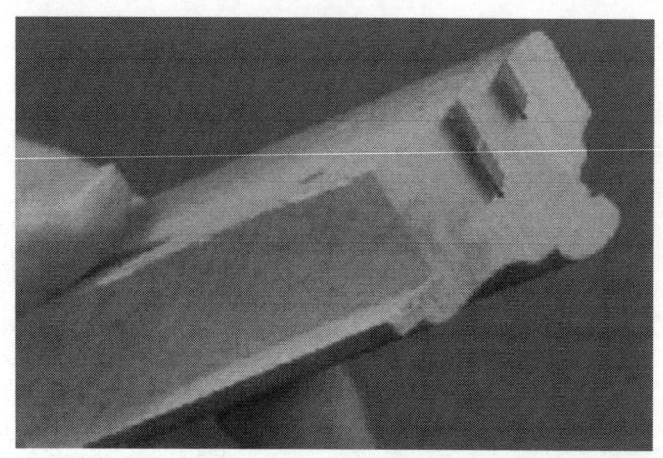

2. Shows wedges in the moulding inserted from below - they can be 'stacked', i.e. One punched in after another to increase the depth of the joint. Each wedge is a 'V' shape with two small flanges; one side has a 'bladed' edge for penetration into the wood.

3. Side view of wedges.

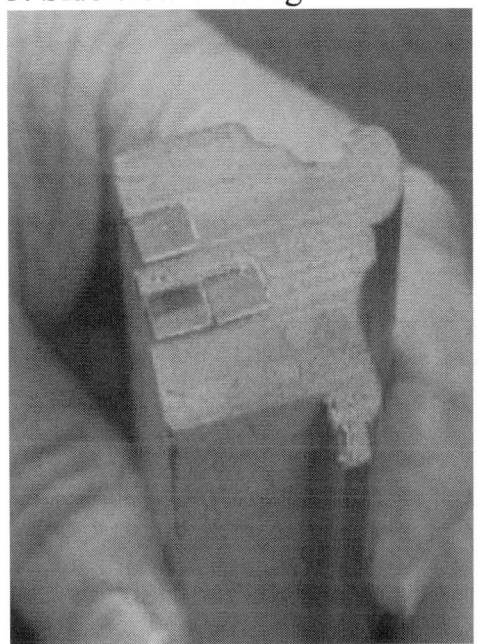

4. Shows 3 wedges in the mitre joint from below.

5. The completed frame.

MACHINE CUTTING A MOUNT

1. The mount cutting machine has the built in facility to trim the outer dimensions of the mount board very accurately.

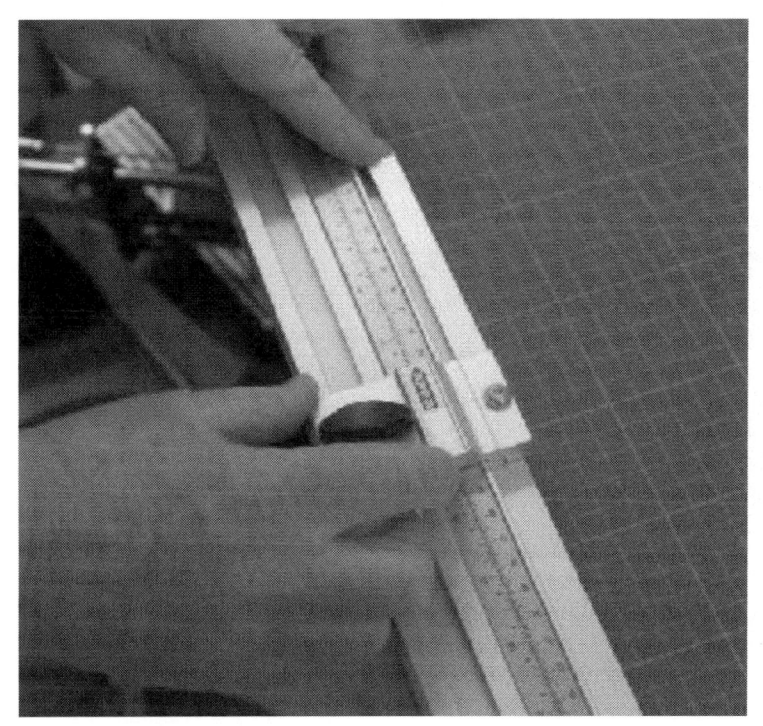

2. Set the calibration.

3. Insert mount board.

4. Trim to size.

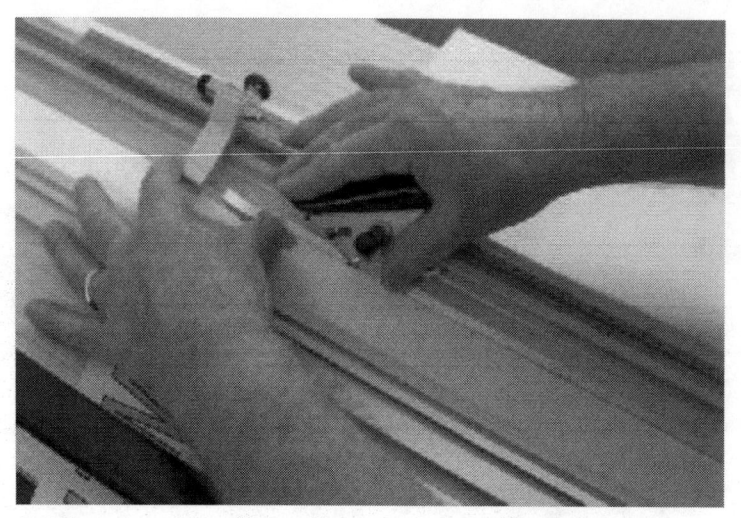

5. Place under slide after setting calibration cut.

6. Shows the cutter head on its sliding bar which lies onto the rear of the mountboard.

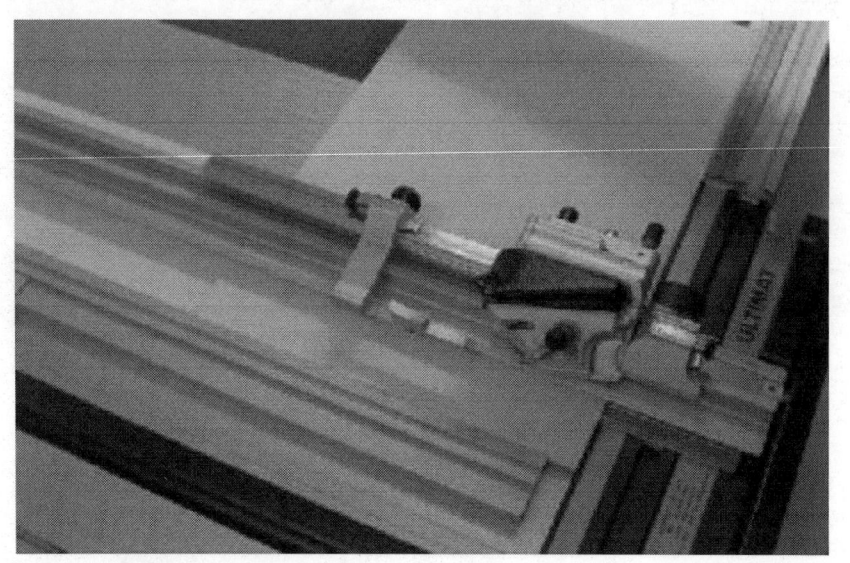

7. Turn the mount board.

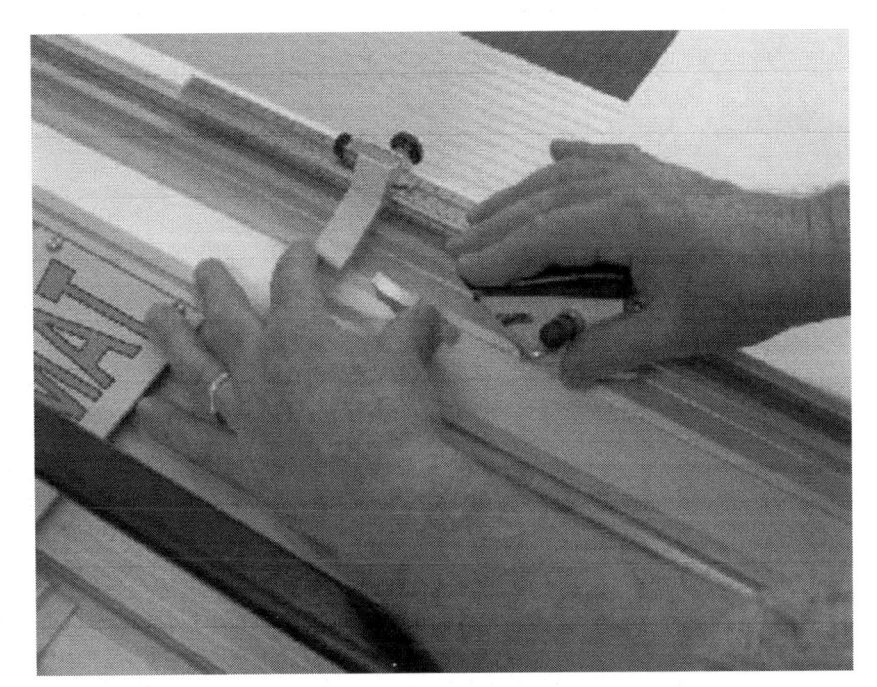

8. Cut.

9. Partially cut mount.

10. The centre 'drops' out.

11. The mount cut and ready for use.

4. Stacking

You should have numerous padded under bench shelves for stacking work in progress. If you put a frame down on the padded surface, you can normally stack anything up to five frames on top but **always** face down and at right angles to one another.

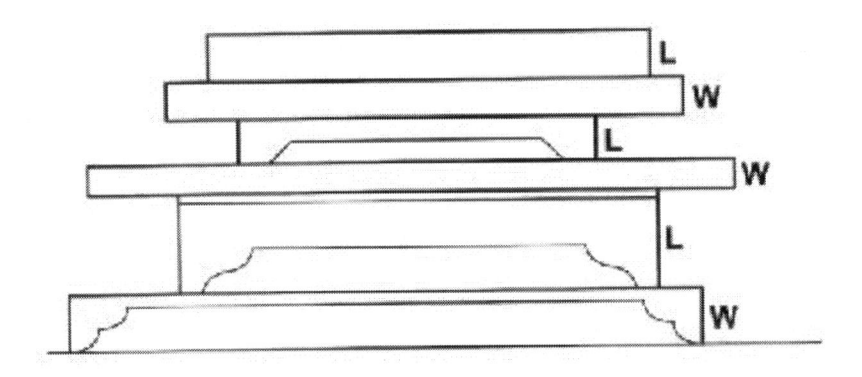

When stacking frames, place face down and alternate length and width. Never slide frames.

Remember to place them down gently. If you slide them they will scratch and damage. If you are worried about damaging them, keep a number of pieces of soft card that can be used as dividers.

5. Mounts

Having made your frames and stacked them to allow the glue to dry, turn your attention to the next process which is the mount cutting. Firstly work out the width of your mount. You will normally do this when you are measuring the picture to write up your job sheet. Modern mount cutting machines work best when you have mounts of even width all round. The old traditional style of mount was to have a bottom margin significantly wider than the other 3 sides. I don't think it is necessary but once again, it works on some pictures.

To obtain this effect on machine cut mounts, make all sides the same width as the bottom then trim the sides and top down to the desire proportions.

The width of the mount is basically determined by what width looks good to enhance the picture. The type of mount used will also determine the dimensions - for instance, double mount, triple mount, wash line mount. The varieties of mount will be dealt with later but for the moment we are concentrating on the basic cutting.

With a mount cutting machine you cut your card to the outside size either with a Stanley knife or guillotine or with the built in cutter on the mount cutting machine. This outer cut must be accurate as the accuracy of the aperture depends on the outer cut.

Once you have your outer measurement, you set the mount cutting machine to the desired width and length of cut and depending on the type of machine cut the two opposite sides or cut in sequence to produce the aperture. These machines cut from the back of the card and work on the principle of a blade in a sliding running block on a bar which lowers onto the moulding. Beware of unnecessary and very unsightly over cuts on the corners!

The other method is hand cutting with various patent cutters and knives - okay if you are doing very few mounts per week but the machining will cut each mount cutting time down to 2 or 3 minutes.

Always store the off-cuts carefully as they will be the material for mounts for smaller pictures. Try to minimise waste. This includes planning how to cut up your larger sheets of card.

Having cut your mounts, put them to one side and move onto the next stage which is glass cutting.

6. Glass Cutting

I use a specific 2mm glass cutter with tungsten carbide wheel which I keep dipped in a little jar containing 50% oil and 50% pure turpentine. (I actually use Extra Virgin Olive Oil from the kitchen! It keeps the cutter wheel in very good condition.)

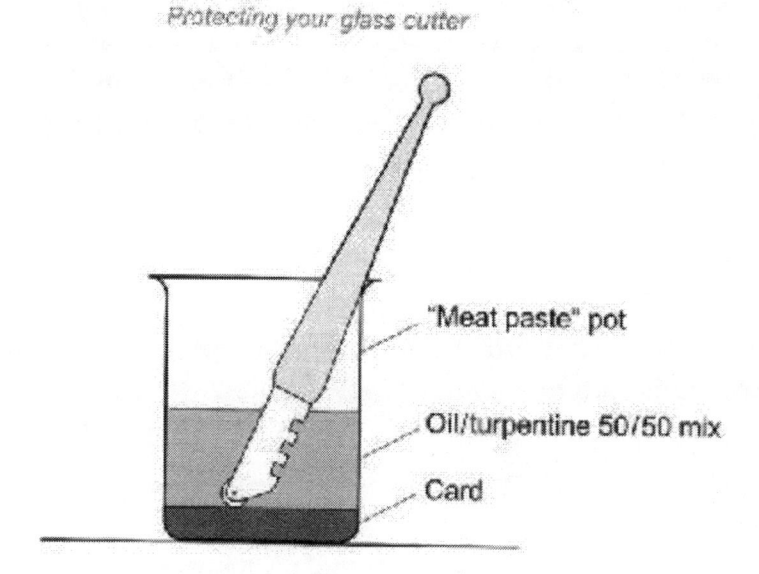

Protecting your glass cutter

- "Meat paste" pot
- Oil/turpentine 50/50 mix
- Card

To mark the glass, I have extra fine fibre tip pens that will write on glass - not the indelible type but one that will give sufficient marking to see and then wipe off easily!

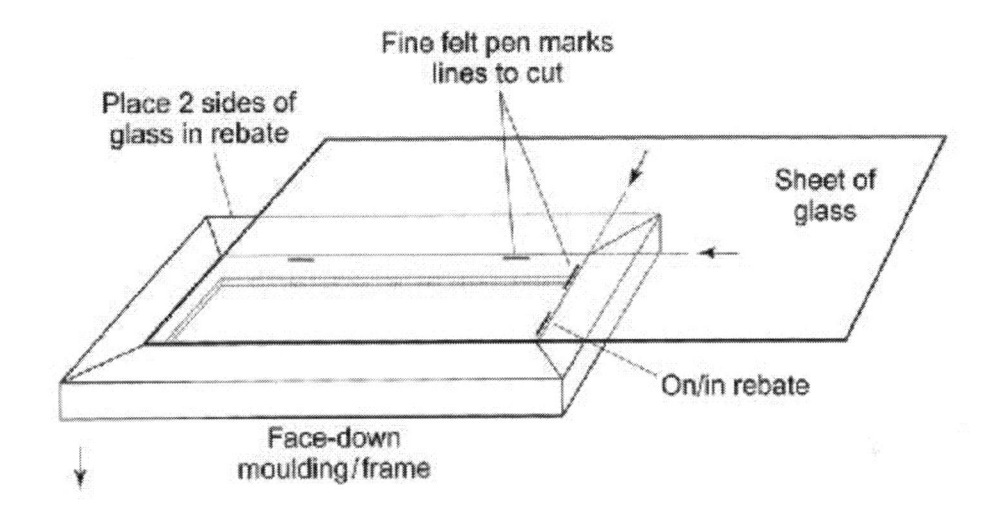

Marking glass for cutting

When starting with a complete sheet of glass, I usually rough cut it to the approximate width of the frame. Do this for the whole sheet so your pieces are more manageable, then carefully place the glass over the frame so that two sides of the glass fit into the length and width rebate of the frame. Mark the glass on the line of the other two sides. Remove the frame and with your square, cut the glass along the marks. Remove the surplus and cut the remaining side. Brush the glass to remove fine splinters and drop into frame. It should fit snugly -though not too tight - so that you can lift it out without effort. A .25 mm gap between glass and end of rebate is ideal.

Cutting glass is very easy but you must be confident. Place your guide on the glass, run the cutter on the glass to produce a single line. If you get the pressure right, the cutter literally "sings" as it runs leaving a fine line. NEVER GO BACK OVER THE LINE: it is a one movement operation. Lift the edge of the glass where the line ends, place the ball end of the cutter under the line and with a short sharp pressure (I put two fingers of one hand on the left hand side and with the fingers of the right hand give a sharp push to the right). With practise, the glass will break cleanly on the line - but not always! A pair of glass pliers will trim off any excess. With practice you will break perfectly 99% of the time!

Breaking scored glass

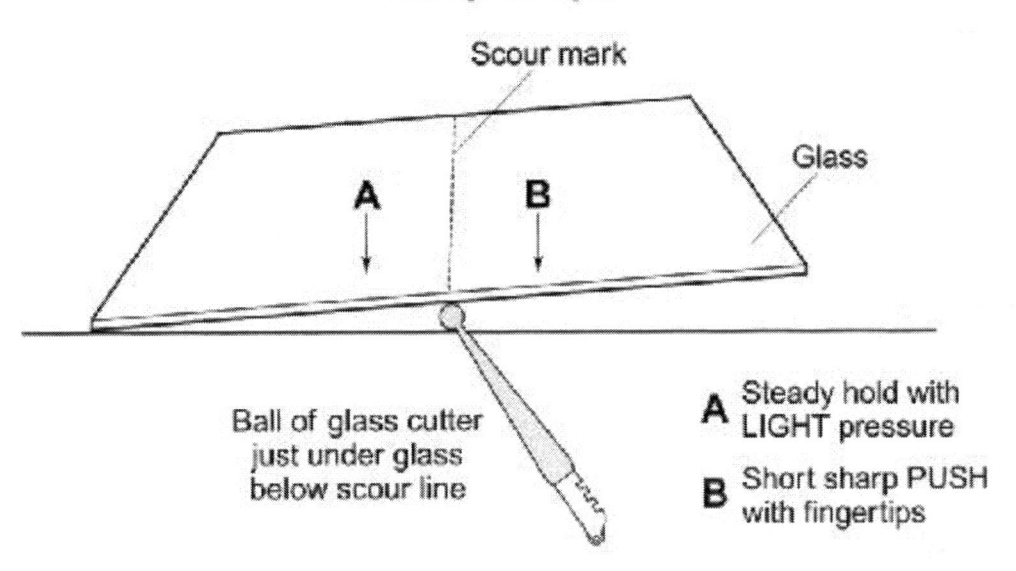

Scour mark

A

B

Glass

Ball of glass cutter just under glass below scour line

A Steady hold with LIGHT pressure

B Short sharp PUSH with fingertips

With longer cuts on larger pieces, once you have scoured the glass, move the sheet over until the scour is just over the edge of the bench and with a short, sharp (but not excessive) tweak, snap off the cut. Once again, practice.

Remember when working with glass to observe the following essential safety guidelines

1. Never slide your hands.

2. Always use deliberate movements.

3. Wear eye protection.

4. Keep other people away from your working area.

It is worth noting at this point that any sliding movements in picture framing should always be avoided. Frames get scratched, so does glass. Always pick up and put down deliberately. Train yourself to do it! In fact this is the most important safety rule: a*lways* use deliberate movements. Never, never slide!

Between each cut, brush the cutting table to minimise splinters - they scratch and damage subsequent sheets of glass! Use a fairly hard brush - the type that is usually sold with a plastic dustpan.

Finally, there are several frameless systems which entail "clipping" the glass, backing and picture together in a sandwich. They were originally invented to help people bypass the cost of framing. The chances are you will never need them but if you do, it will be necessary to "de-edge" your glass. To do this is very simple.

Cut the glass and then placing the edge of the glass on the end of the bench, take off the sharp portion by rubbing gently with a small oilstone until it is rounded and safe.

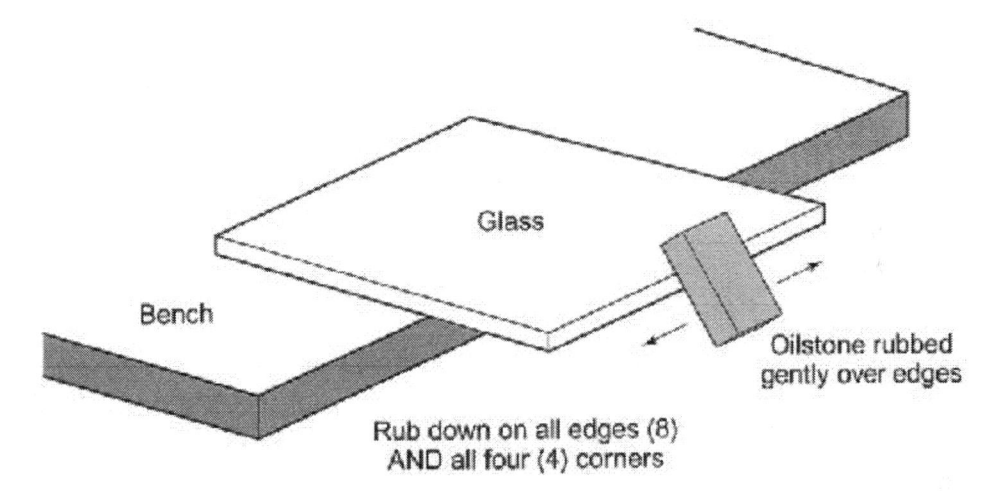

De-edging the glass

Repeat the process for all eight sharp edges on the sheet and give the corners a rub at the end. This produces a "safe" piece of glass.

7. Backing Board

The final piece of the framing jigsaw is the backing board which is cut to fit the rear of the frame - once again a lose fit to allow for expansion and contraction. Cut the board on the guillotine (if you have one, or if not, with a craft knife) and using the glass in the frames to act as a template, mark your board with a pencil prior to cutting. Once again, plan your cuts to minimise waste and store your off-cuts for use on smaller frames.

You now have your frame, made with its joints pinned and glued, waiting within is the glass and backing and your mounts are cut, so it time to start the final phase - assembly and finishing.

CUTTING GLASS

Offer glass up to frame and mark the two edges for cutting with a fine felt pen.

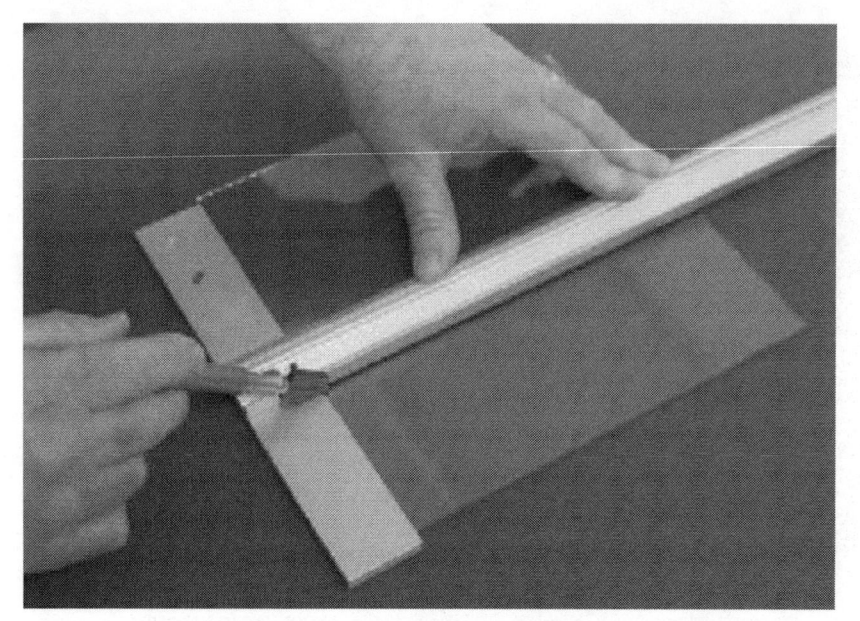

Place rule on glass and run cutter over the glass (once only - make it sing!)

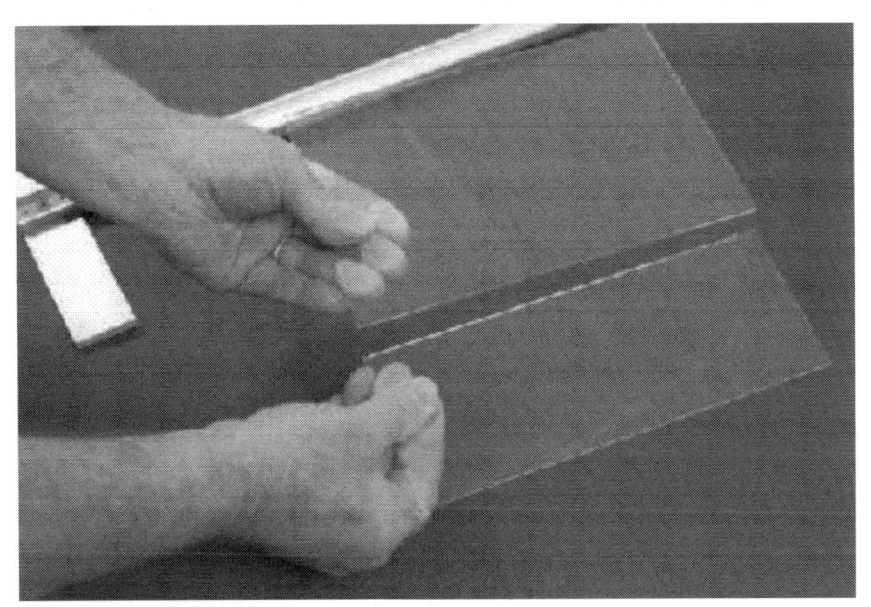

With a positive action, snap along the line, like this on a small piece or on the bench edge or with the 'ball' on the end of the glass cutter wheel.

ASSEMBLING THE FRAME

You now have the component parts of your picture frames made and ready for assembly.

Firstly, clean the glass on both sides. Cleaning the glass requires a very good glass cleaner. I use a specific cleaner called "Nilglass" which my wholesaler sells. It does not leave smears. I have two dusters (well worn without excess fluff), one to apply the cleaner the other to polish.

Clean both sides and then hold up to the light to check for missed areas or ot her marks. Good glass cleaning is absolutely vital and you should endeavour to wash your cleaning cloths frequently.

Once satisfied that your glass is clean, put the backing board into the frame to protect the glass.

It is at this point that I should mention the tide marks that occasionally appear on the glass when wet. These are ripples of pattern that appear in the surface and mystified me for many years - and drew blank stares from the glass suppliers. I eventually found the cause. When the glass is delivered, it is often separated by sheets of paper - like thin newsprint - to protect the glass. If left between the glass this paper absorbs moisture and the acid in the paper "etches" the surface of the glass. It is very annoying and since I pointed it out to my supplier, a problem of the past. I have nonetheless noticed the paper between the glass in other glaziers and framers so it is best to remove it when the glass is delivered.

Having cleaned the glass, it is time to prepare the mount. Make sure they fit the frame snugly (don't forget room to expand and contract) and if required, put double mounts together.

You are now ready to take the pictures out of storage and put them into the frames. I tend to put them all in place ready for the final assembly, in other words, trim, fit them in mounts and put backing on the pictures where necessary.

To assemble, start with the frame in front of you. Lift out the backing so you are l eft with the moulding frame and glass. Switch on the vacuum, which ideally will plug into the front of the bench with an easy access switch. On the long hose, using a clean circular brush head that is kept specifically for this purpose, brush and dust the glass and the inside of the rebate. Dust the front of the picture and mount and carefully place them in the frame. Then dust the backing board and place on top. Run the brush round the slight gap between contents and moulding, replace the brush and switch off the vacuum cleaner. Put the frame against the stop bar and put two pins in on each side, near the mitre.

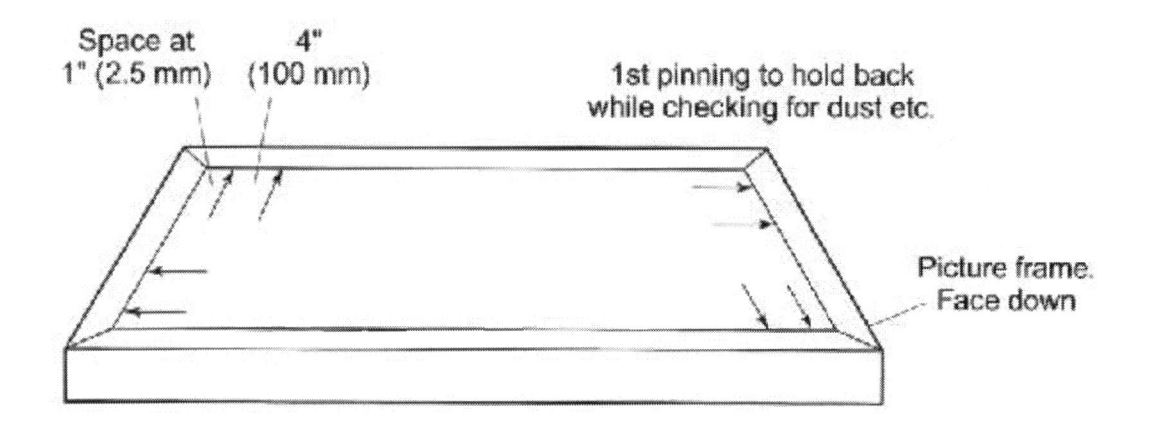

Space at 1" (2.5 mm)

4" (100 mm)

1st pinning to hold back while checking for dust etc.

Picture frame. Face down

Carefully lift up the frame and make sure that there are no dust flecks trapped under the glass and that the mount and picture all sit straight. I have an old set of dividers (out of a geometry set) to ensure all is even. If all is well, replace the frame on the bench and complete the pinning of the back. I place my darts/pins at about 10cm (4in.) Intervals. Turn the frame over and check for damage, inaccuracies, dust. Be very critical as you want perfection! If there is a problem, you can put it right before you start taping up. Repeat the process with all the frames you are making.

Making Good

There will often be production marks on the spine of the moulding at the mitres. These are clamp marks and counter sunk panel pin holes and occasionally chipping to the moulding caused by the downward pressure of the guillotine on the spine.

Remember there should be no damage to the face of the moulding - if there is reject the entire frame and re-cut. You can never match up and in the long run it is cheaper and better for your reputation to have a perfect frame. You can always re-cut and re-use the reject frame at a later date. Any production marks should be filled. I use Brummers Interior Stopping in white or cream made by Clam Brummer - a paste that does not shrink, adheres well, excess can be wiped off with a damp cloth, it can be fine sanded and takes colour well. I then cover this with Wax Gilt matched to the moulding finish or if it is coloured, I use artists acrylic mixed in very small amounts and matched to the frame colour but remember, too little rather than too much! I mix the acrylics on glass off-cuts and with care can get a perfect match.

Taping Up

Taping up is the sealing of the rear of the frame to prevent dust entering. There are many makes of pre-gummed sticky tape on the market, usually of a plastic nature. (I've even seen brown plastic packaging tape used!) I would only recommend one method and that is the traditional brown paper tape which is pre glued and requires wetting to stick it to the frame (hereafter called "gum strip"), the main reason being it can be completely and cleanly removed (even years on) by simply wetting the tape, waiting for the glue to soften and peeling it off. Any glue on the moulding wipes off with a damp cloth.

I carry 4cm, 5cm and 7.5cm (1.½in., 2in. and 3in.) wide rolls on dispensers fixed under the shelf. These pull out and cut to size - 8mm (¼in.) shorter than the frame. They are then placed on a hardboard off-cut approximately 1m x 20cm (3ft 3in. x 8in.) and wet using a 5cm (2in.) decorators brush with water in a dog's plastic water (non spill!) bowl. First, place the tape along the two short sides of the frame then along the long sides. Position carefully, wipe smooth and leave to dry overnight.

Some framers do fiddly mitre cuts at the corners - frankly if you place the tape neatly, it is a waste of time. The only real variation on the proceeding assembly system is for open glassless frames such as oils on canvas and in the case of these I like to first line the back of the moulding and rebate with gum strip paper. Once it has dried, put the canvas with its stretcher into the rebate and fix in place using one of the patent systems or by tapping in a panel pin at an angle and bending it over the back of the canvas to hold it in place. These can then be twisted aside to take out the canvas. (Take care over how deep you insert the nails - don't go right through the face of the moulding!)

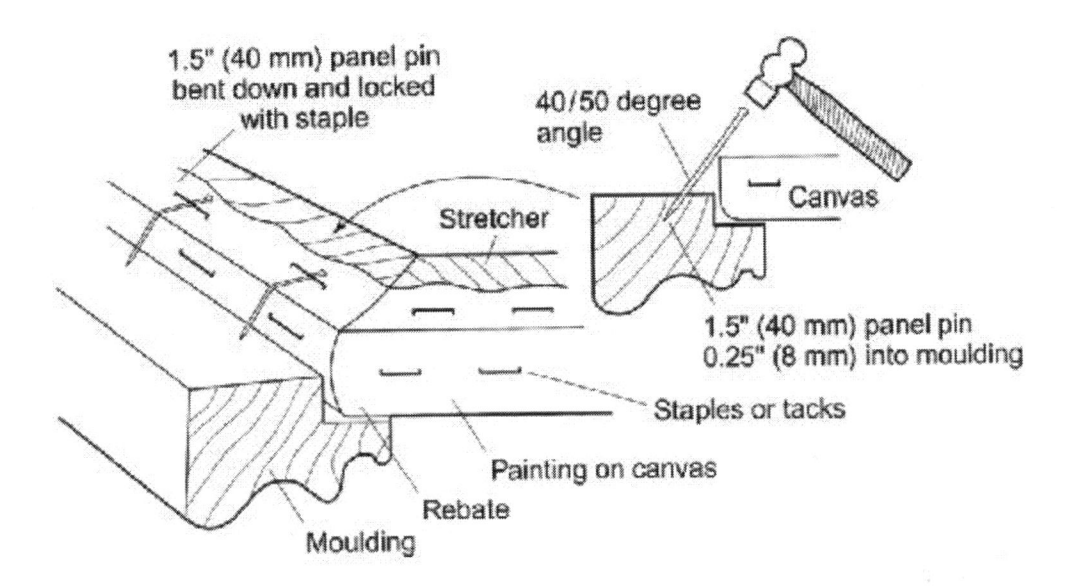

Diagram labels:
- 1.5" (40 mm) panel pin bent down and locked with staple
- 40/50 degree angle
- Canvas
- Stretcher
- 1.5" (40 mm) panel pin 0.25" (8 mm) into moulding
- Staples or tacks
- Painting on canvas
- Rebate
- Moulding

Before bending the pin over, place a piece of tape on the canvas (to protect the canvas from rust should the pin corrode) and then put a couple of easily removed wire staples across the pin to lock it in place. I always cover the back of the canvas with a thin card panel taped to the moulding to offer the rear of the picture (canvas) protection from dust etc.

Finally, you will frequently get pictures to frame that have dedications or information labels, or pictures to re-frame that have valuable information on the original frame. Rather than just "stick" this on the backing, I always cut and clean an off-cut of glass that adequately covers the relevant information. I then place this on the backing board and fix it in place with gum strip paper when I am taping up the back of the picture. It is always well received by the customer!

Fixing, Hangings & Frame Furniture

The final process of assembly is the fitting of the furniture, which are the hangings.

Hanging furniture is either eyes, rings on eyes or D-rings in the moulding. Other hangings rivet onto the backing board. The rule of thumb is that hangings are fixed of the distance from the top of the frame. You then have the choice of non stretch cord or wire. I use multi strand brass wire with a steel core in one of three sizes, between screwed in D-rings. Once again, appearance is important so tie the cord neatly or in the case of wire, twist it neatly up to the ring. A bit of practise and you should have a neat finish (a bit like a hangman's noose or a whipped rope end). There is one thing to remember here and that is the hangings on the back of a frame can cause awful damage to the front of a frame when stacked, so if you are bespoke framing for shops, or agents, make the holes in the moulding to accept screws/eyes but don't fix them. Rather place a couple of screw eyes and a length of wire neatly coiled onto the backing, secured with sellotape. This should reduce the chances of the frame being damaged in the shop. I had a rubber stamp (the simple self inking type of machine) that said "PLEASE ENSURE RINGS AND WIRE SECURE BEFORE HANGING" which I stamped on the back of every frame to make sure the customer took care over hanging.

Finally wrap your pictures well. I always take a large enough sheet of Kraft paper off the roll, place it on the bench, cut a piece of bubble pack the same size as the frame, place this on the Kraft paper then put the frame face down on top. Fold the paper over and tape up. If I have to stack or load a client's car, I always put the frames in pairs, face to face, back to back and tell the customer how to look after his or her frames. You are the expert and that includes making sure they get their frames home and hung without mishap!

Back

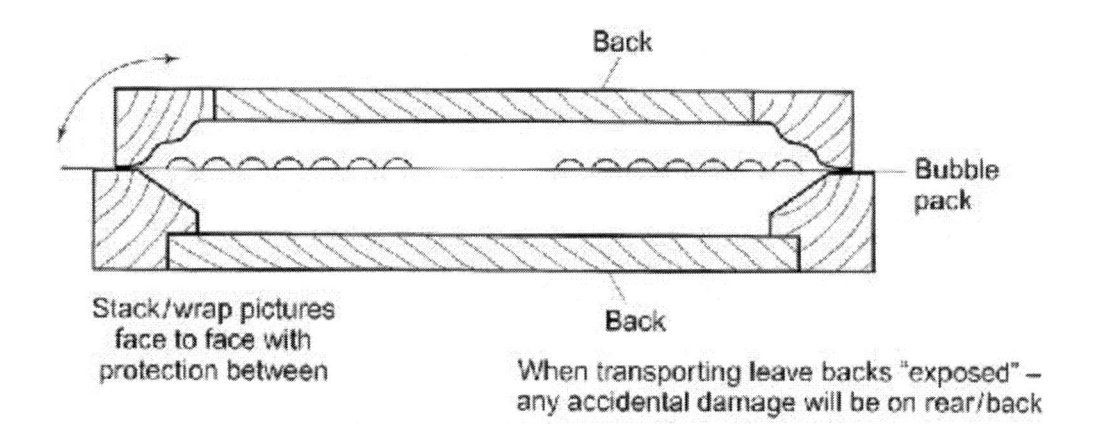

Bubble pack

Back

Stack/wrap pictures face to face with protection between

When transporting leave backs "exposed" – any accidental damage will be on rear/back

SELLING YOURSELF AND YOUR FRAMING

PRICING

The following is the calculation I use to obtain my price charts. They are designed to give an accurate quote at the outset. I then fill out an order slip (I buy the basic order books with triplicate sheets and stamp my address on the top). I write down a detailed description of what has been chosen and add the quote. I give a copy to the customer as proof of my having their picture and the choice made so there is never any dispute as to who said what. If you are framing for local shops, supply them with an order book which has a copy for the customer, copy for themselves and a copy for you. Remember that the more people there are in the chain, the more risk of misunderstanding - if it is in writing, you are covered.

Calculating your price

When calculating your picture frame prices, you will require a price based on a small unit, i.e. square centimetre (or square inch). Having established a small price, you can then multiply it up on each frame to the area or length of that individual frame.

The picture frame cost breaks down to three pricing components:

1. Moulding - linear price

2. Glass / Mount /Backing - square price

3. Sundries - static price.

In other words, the moulding price is calculated on the linear price of the moulding; glass, mount and backing are calculated on the square metre price; sundries are priced on the quantity of hangings which tend to be the same for all frames. Or to put it another way, divide the moulding price by the length, i.e., if you buy 30 metres of moulding at £X, divide the £X by 30 then by 100 to obtain the price per centimetre run of moulding. As for glass, mount board and backing take the individual costs of each and divide the each figure by the number of sheets. Having calculated the price of a sheet, measure the sheet to ca lculate how many square centimetres in that sheet then divide the sheet price by this figure giving you a price per square centimetre.

The sundries tend to have a basic price throughout, so all you have to do is list the necessary components: Pins, glue, fastenings, hangings, glass cleaner, tape, filler. You will use roughly the same amount of the above on every frame therefore use the on price - for example, if you use 5p of material on each of the above, the total would be 35p and therefore I would use a figure of 50p to ensure that all sundry costs are more that adequately covered.

Having calculated the above, you can now work out the unit pr ice. The concept of this price list is worked on the sum of two sides of the picture to be framed, i.e. the length and the width, which gives you a complete price. It is tedious to calculate but once done, will enable you to give your customer an on the spot quote that you can be sure will be accurate.

Start with the moulding. Take the minimum size of frame you want to make - I use 15cm x 10cm (6" x 4"). Add these two figures together then multiply by the centimetre length price of the moulding. Continue adding 1cm to the length and multiplying by the centimetre length price,

i.e. 25cm x Price Y
26cm x Price Y
27cm x Price Y

until you reach the maximum picture size you think you will be making - my price list goes up to 230cms (90"). Each moulding in your stock has to be calculated this way but to make life easier, your stock can be grouped into categories based on price. I use Groups A - D, for example, Group A - 5p, B - 10p, C - 20p, D - 25p.

Mount board is then multiplied up on the same principle, i.e. 15 x 10 = 25 sq. cms x 1 sq. cm price

To make this calculation easier, draw up a lined page thus:

Length of 2 sides	Moulding Price	Glass Price	Mount Price	Backing Price	Sundries Price	Total

Note that the above is calculated on the size of the picture. However, if a mount is required, the size of the frame is increased and you must therefore allow for this (and other extras) by adding on the double width of the mount to cover the additional mount board, backing and glass used. To calculate this, measure the picture, decide on the width of the mount and double - for e xample a 10cm x 20cm picture (total of 30cm) with a 10cm wide mount will become 20cm x 30cm, giving a total of 50 to read off against the price list.

Having calculated the above, you have your cost price list. Now decide your mark-up and add this on, producing an identical design of price list for your retail price. If you are trade framing, produce a third version which will be your Trade price list. Don't mix them up!

Sample Price List

X2 Sides	Price Band 5p per cm	Price Band 10p per cm	Price Band 15p per cm	Price Band 20p per cm
10	£5.02	£7.60	£10.19	£12.77
11	£5.27	£8.12	£10.96	£13.61
12	£5.53	£8.63	£11.74	£14.84

Having produced your basic price list then calculate a unit price for the other services you provide, e.g. tapestry stretching, embroidery stretching, canvas stretching, decorated mounts. These costs should be added to the reference section along with those for double mounts, non reflecting glass etc., so that you are able to give an accurate price on the spot. For double or triple mounts add a fixed amount per extra sheet of mount board, and the same for non reflecting glass.

For a frame only order, take only the linear price of the frame, add on the sundries amount then multiply up to include your mark up.

Once you have calculated your price list, you will notice a large differential on the prices between Group A and Group D. This is brought about by the far higher prices of the large mouldings. Your profits therefore jump hugely on the larger moulding, but the extra cost will also deter many customers from using these mouldings.

However, the time taken to make a frame is the same irrespective of the size of the moulding. To take account of this you may wish to adjust your profit percentage on each group, i.e. if you decide on a general mark up of 100%, Group A (the cheapest) might be marked up 150% and Group D (the most expensive) might be reduced to 75% to adequately cover your labour costs at the bottom end of the scale and to make the expensive mouldings more attractive at the top.

Also bear in mind the following three points.

1. When calculating the unit price, include VAT if you are not registered but leave this out if you are
registered as you claim the VAT back and charge VAT on the total framing price.
2. Mark the maximum size for any thickness of frame when doing price lists for agents. If you don't, you will find people ordering 1.83m x 1.22m (6ft x 4ft) frames with 15mm (½") moulding in an effort to get themselves a bargain!
3. Mark up is the amount you make on top of the cost of material. It must include waste, plus all of your overheads and finally your profit.

You must be mindful of the going rate for picture framing. You do not want to overprice as custom will drift to the opposition whilst at the same time to undercut too dramatically will undermine your sustainability of your business. To find out the going rate, I usually wander into a framer out of my area and give them the size of an imaginary picture and ask for a quote. Do this for a variety of frames and you will soon get an idea on the going rate. Do not worry too much about the ethics of "spying" because everyone does it. Keeping an eye on the opposition is fairly normal practice!

An old shopkeeper gave me a couple of tips that I have never forgotten. The first is that as long as you make a penny more than you paid, you have made a profit because profit is what is in the bank, not decorating the walls. The second is never lose a customer. Once a person has decided to visit your shop or gallery, the object is to sell them something. For this you have to watch the customer and apply a degree of psychology. When you give the quote, watch their reaction. If they think it is too much they usually look startled, say they'll think about it and flee to the opposition. Offer them discount - remember a bit of discount goes a long way - and they are usually so pleased that they return. Return or repeat custom is the core of your business.

The world divides into two categories - people who have things framed and those that never do! You will find that once you have a satisfied customer, they return time after time and strangely at roughly the same intervals - with me it is every couple of months on average. These people will be your bread and butter and given the service they expect, will be very loyal. (However you will always notice a slight variation in trade when a new framer starts in the area -there are always a few who rush off to try the new opposition!)

Remember when pricing for shops they require their mark up, so you must allow for them to increase your price from 33 % to 50%. For volume trade framing, you will make pennies per frame. However, these orders run into hundreds of the same size frame. It is boring work but added to the whole is grist to the profits mill. Beware of the individual who will come in with one picture, get a quote and then demands a substantial discount on the one picture because he has dozens or even hundreds more. I always reply that when he brings in the volume framing, he can have the discount.

The clear advantage with picture framing as a business is that you are in possession of their frame. 90% of customers pay on collection but some however will pick up the frame and mutter to send them the bill. I never allow the frame to leave until I have been paid. The same applies to the shop trade custom. They have the samples, they take the order, the customer collects the frame and pays them, therefore they have no risk or outlay, so paying on delivery is quite fair. There are a certain class of customer that are bad payers - the money is in the post or they will bring it round and it never arrives and when they do pay, they make you feel that you are taking food from their children's mouths. I do not do business with them as they are more stress than profit.

On the other hand you may get large companies coming to you for frames. They normally have an accounting system of 30, 60 or 90 days payment which you have to accept - although they are generally good for the money!

FINDING CUSTOMERS

The very best source of custom is word of mouth and recommendation. If you have a shop or visible signed premises, passing trade will produce results. If you have a back garden workshop, you are going to have to find ways of getting known. I have found advertising in local papers and magazines expensive with very little return. The most effective publicity I found was visiting shops - be they galleries, gift shops antique shops, cafes - and giving them my business card.

Visit the local art clubs they of ten have members who make frames but you will always find half a dozen or more members who like to be different. Offering the club a substantial discount often helps.

Contact your local post office. They do leaflets with the post, usually a minimum of 5000 leaflets. If there are large businesses in your area, a letter to their Managing Director, introducing yourself with a few business cards pays dividends as does doing leaflets yourself. When I first started, I would visit housing estates or villages and spend a couple of hours pushing nicely produced leaflets or business cards through their letter boxes. Do the same for industrial units.

Schools, colleges and courses that give out certificates are worth targeting too.

Don't dash off and spend all your time publicizing yourself. Rather set a target, say 2 hours per week, to target one area or estate.

ASPECTS OF FRAMING

MOULDING

The range of mouldings is huge. The normal practice is to buy the moulding ready made from the wholesaler. You can, however, produce your own.

You can buy milled timber moulding without any finish and decorate and finish it to your own taste, using stains, colours, varnishes and various metallic and gold leaf finishes.

My tutor who was of the old school of framers, told me of his 7 years apprenticeship under a picture framer. He produced individual frames by making up the frame in a basic wooden moulding then would carve a design into the moulding with chisels, then guild and varnish the frame, applying an antique finish with a final distressing, producing a stunningly beautiful and stunningly expensive frame! You do not have to be so lavish and your best bet is to experiment by buying ready cut profiles and applying different finishes - artists' acrylic paints can be very effective. (In this regard, see also the separate chapter in this section on gilding.)

Swept frames are mouldings made up into frames. A decorative moulding is then applied to the corners and along the sides then sections are cut out and pierced to give you the swept frame effect.

Applied decoration pinned/glued onto frame

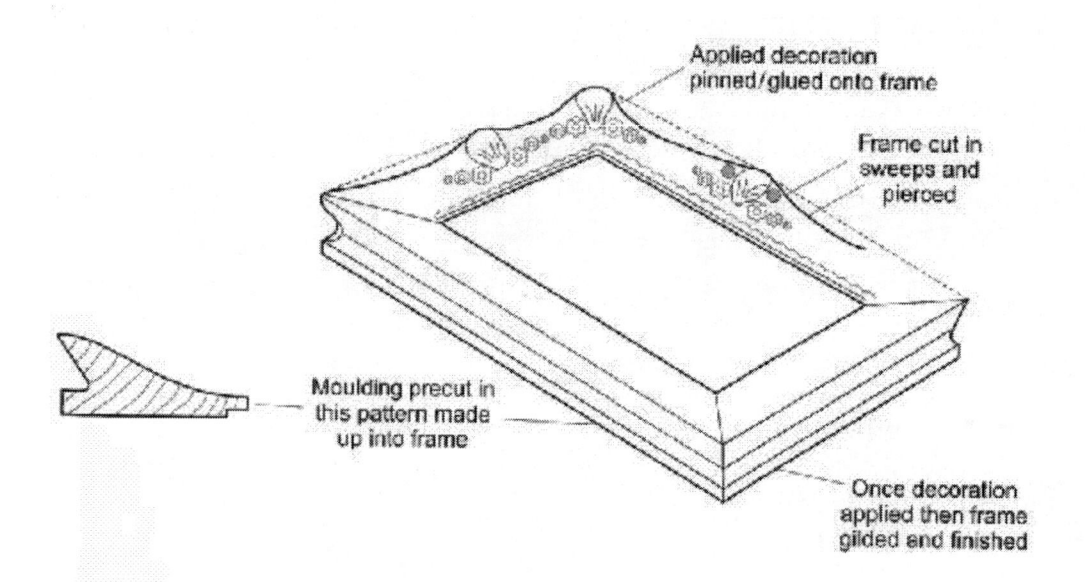

Frame cut in sweeps and pierced

Moulding precut in this pattern made up into frame

Once decoration applied then frame gilded and finished

Swept frame

These frames are produced in large quantities in the Far East to standard sizes and are so go od that I frankly do not feel it is worth making them. What I have found rewarding is to individualize frames by gluing designs of my own onto a wooden moulding base. To do this, I use a children's modelling dough which is sculpted or cut to the shape I want, glued to the frame and coated with "patent" gesso. Gesso is a mixture of "rabbit skin glue and whiting" and mercifully there are now numerous pre prepared gessoes. This is then gilded and finished to produce some very pleasing frames that are unique and long lasting (those I made 25 years ago still look as good as new).

I occasionally play around with individual frames but my experience is that they are costly to produce, time consuming and in the UK rarely profitable. If you are framing to make money, stick to the ready made.

Slip Frames

These are flat mouldings cut to fit within the rebate of the outer frame, either to widen it for aesthetic appeal or for practical reasons, e.g. the painting being framed has a wide unsightly margin or a spacer is needed between glass and picture.

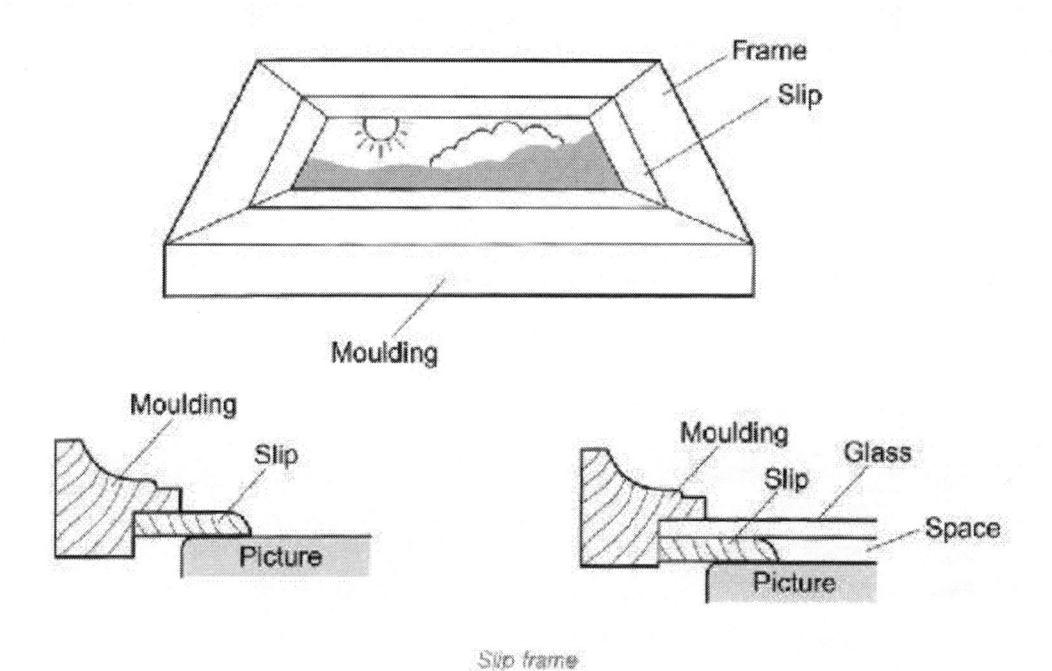

Slip frame

Oval Frames

These mouldings are like "swept frames" in that they are produced in standard sizes in a variety of finishes. Making ovals is both costly and time consuming. I find that a good supplier's catalogue with photos of their range of ovals is sufficient. The rare customer who wants an oval is usually happy to wait a few days. However, if you have a shop or workshop with good public access, I find it worthwhile to carry a range of swept frames and ovals - they tend to inspire customers but only stock them once you have an established trade. Do not tie up money in slow moving stock!

Box Frames (shadow boxes/frames)

These are frames that contain either a 3 dimensional object or require the subject to be set back from the glass. A box frame at its simplest is an outer frame with glass fitted in its rebate. A second frame (for this I use one of 3 ramin wood mouldings, painted to the required colour with artists' acrylics) is then fitted into the rebate, holding the glass and giving a second rebate for the subject and backing.

3 Ramin mouldings. Ideal for box frames

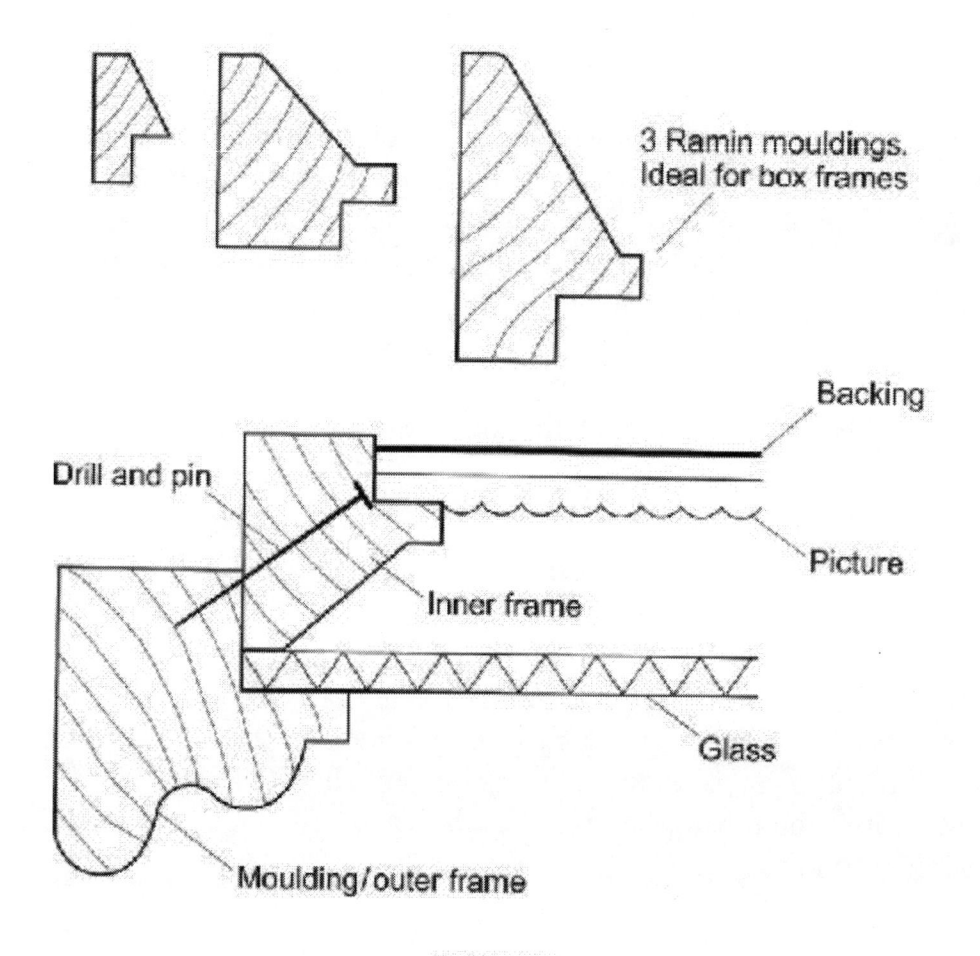

Backing
Drill and pin
Picture
Inner frame
Glass
Moulding/outer frame

Box frame

You can achieve a similar effect using mount board. You have the visible mount behind the glass and then several sheets of card - cut with a wider aperture than the first mount board - fitted behind, then the subject, creating a space between glass, mount and picture.

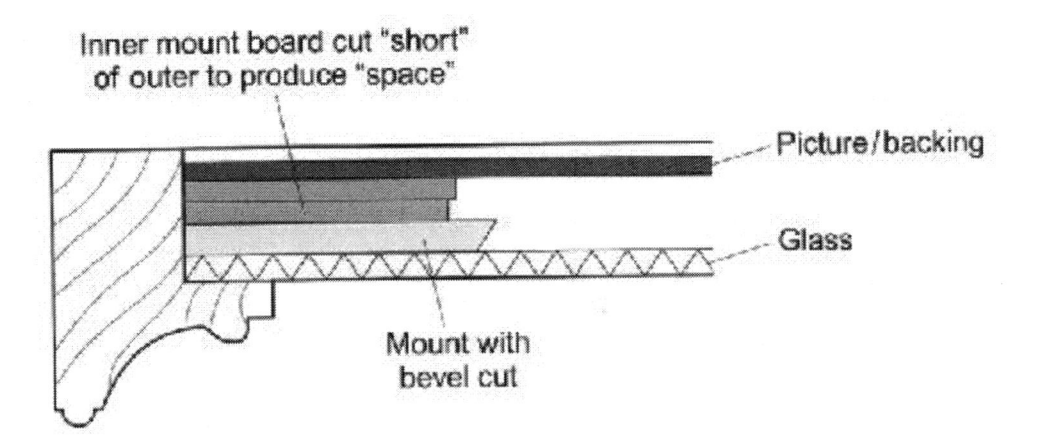

Creating 'space' using mount board

Double Frames

Double frames are normally two sizes of the same moulding, the outer, a decorated panel and then the inner holding the subject.

The easiest method is to make the outer frame, cut a hardboard to fit, cut out the centre of the hardboard allowing a lip to fix the inner frame which is screwed to the hardboard giving two frames with a hardboard surround which can be decorated (NB decorate the hardboard panel before fixing the frames!).

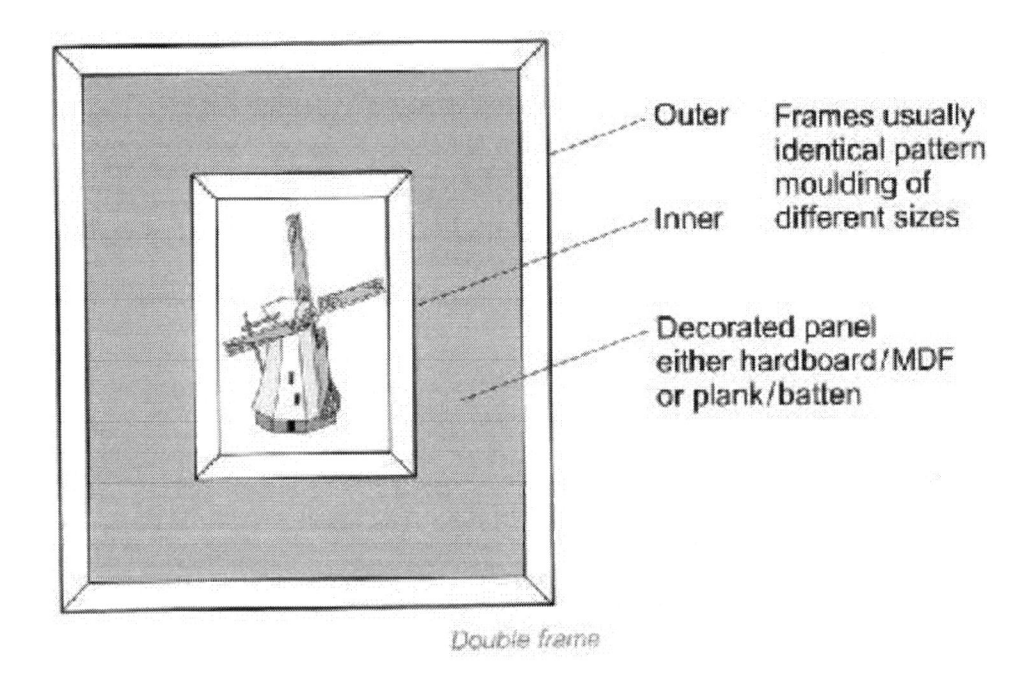

Outer
Inner

Frames usually identical pattern moulding of different sizes

Decorated panel either hardboard/MDF or plank/batten

Double frame

I recently made was for a hotel that had very striking wallpaper on vast walls. The prints they h ad chosen were large but still looked small on the wall, so we made the double frames with their chosen wallpaper in-between, creating large and very striking pictures.

Mirror Frames

Basically mirrors are framed as you would any other panel type subject. If you are framing mirrors to sell on spec., buy bevelled mirrors that will look very good in their frames. Hanging is with mirror plates to stop them getting knocked off the wall and to keep them flat on the wall so they can be looked into. There are also several designs of secret hangings to fix mirror frames to walls.

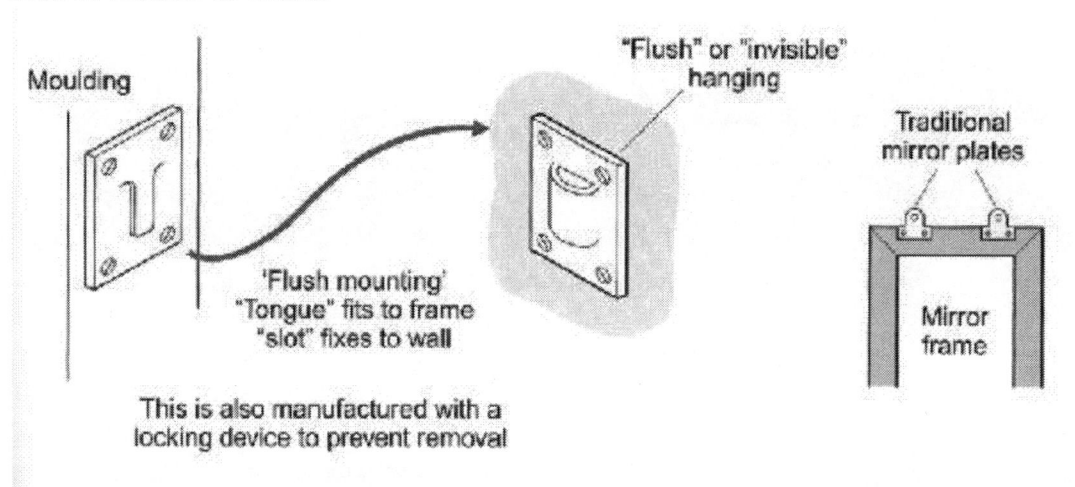

There is one rule when framing mirrors that must be followed - blacken the rebate. If you look at the edge of a framed mirror you will see the reflection of the back of the rebate, which is unsightly. When framing mirrors therefore, it is important that after you have made the frame, you blacken the inside of the rebate with artists' black acrylic - or felt pen or stain.

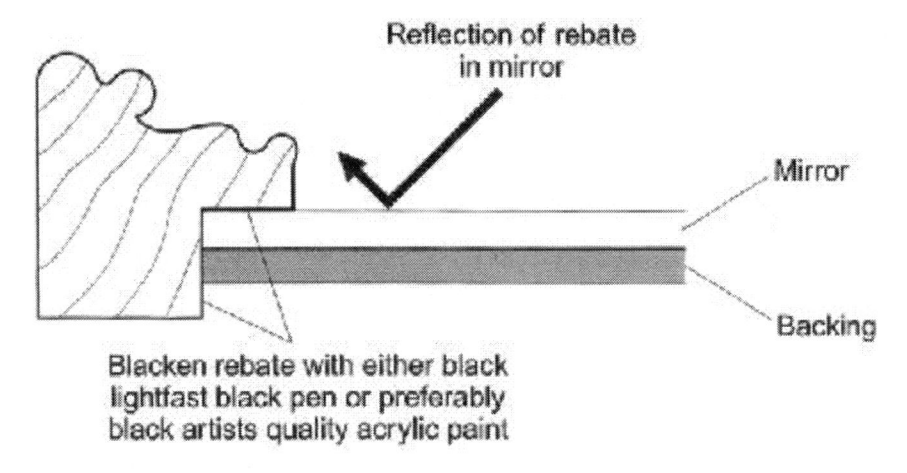

Reflection of rebate in mirror

Mirror

Backing

Blacken rebate with either black lightfast black pen or preferably black artists quality acrylic paint

PROFILES

Moulding patterns are normally classified by the supplier with their references. I always re-number them with my own system, i.e. AF/one, AF/two to simplify my sample board - and to stop people from finding my source of moulding easily! However, it is worth knowing the names given to general styles of moulding:

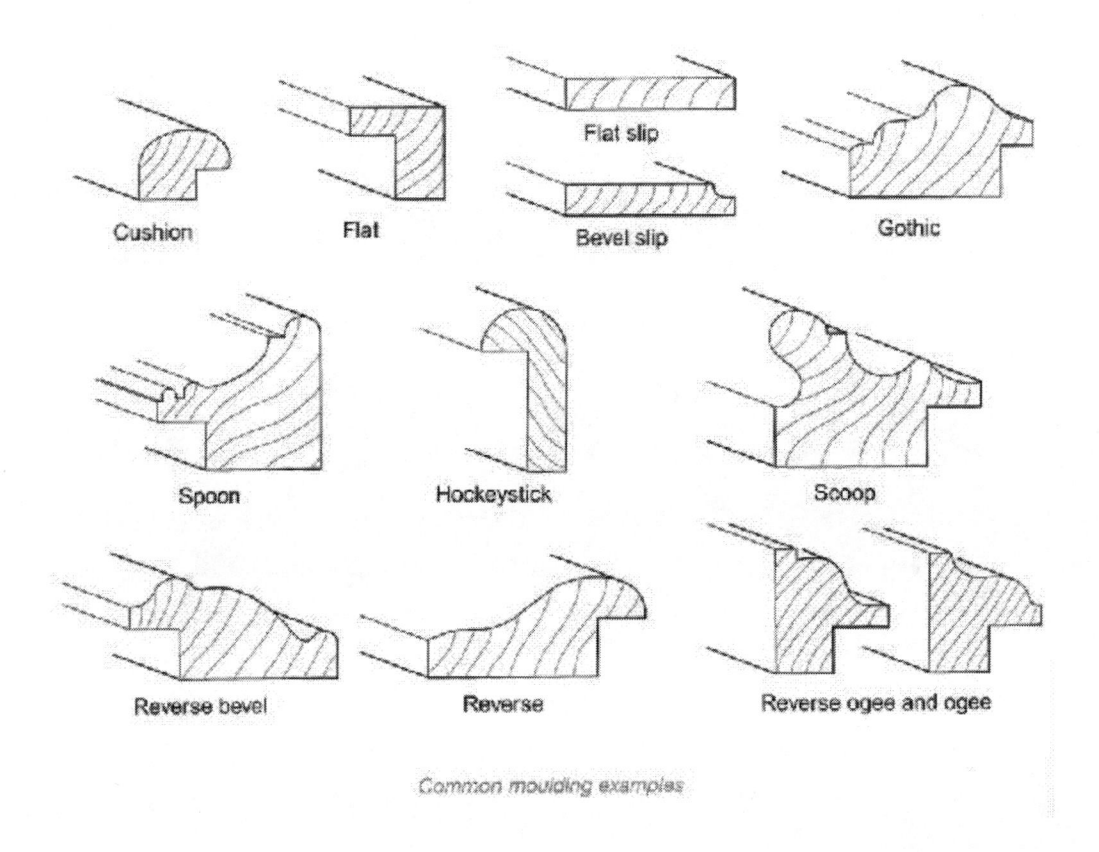

Common moulding examples

MOUNTS, MATTS AND MOUNT BOARD

As I explained earlier, the mount is for decorative enhancement and separation from the glass. There are literally hundreds of colours and textures of mount boards, giving you an endless range of combinations. The limit is your imagination. One tip is not to overstate your mounts. Remember you are complimenting the subject, not dominating or completely overwhelming it. Interestingly you will frequently get customers who want a red sunset framed in red to go with their red wallpaper or maroon carpet. My experience is that they have a picture they want framed. If you frame the picture in a way that will enhance the picture it will normally fit in with their decor, no matter how bizarre! You will, however, frequently get carpet samples, wallpaper and curtains all to be matched to the framing!

Mounts fall into several categories:

Single Mount

The simplest, this is a single cut out sheet to surround the picture.

Multiple Mount

The next type is the multiple mount, which is several sheets of different colours, or tones, or textures, cut with increased aperture to produce an outer colour with bands of varying colour to the subject, giving an increased depth and leading the eye into the frame and its subject. You can have double, triple or multiple mounts but remember the depth of your moulding rebate - it might need to be very deep! Also there is no hard and fast rule as to the width of overlap - what looks best will vary from one picture to the next.

Multiple mounts are held together using a single length of double sided tape. Ensure accuracy using your dividers.

Decorated Mounts

The next category is the decorated mount and you will find an endless array of decorated tape banding pre prepared in a variety of designs for you to apply to your mount. The traditional mount decoration is called "wash line" mounts which is basically a series of delicate lines drawn onto the mat with a delicate colour wash between two or several of the lines.

Wash Line Mounts

To produce wash line mounts, you will need:
a) draughtsman's ruling pen
b) straight edge rule with a raised lip to keep the ruler and wet ink apart
c) very fine pin

d) card off-cut to check your colours and the flow of pen and brush
e) fine pointed brush - size 3, 4 or 5
f) pencil (sharp)
g) pair of dividers.

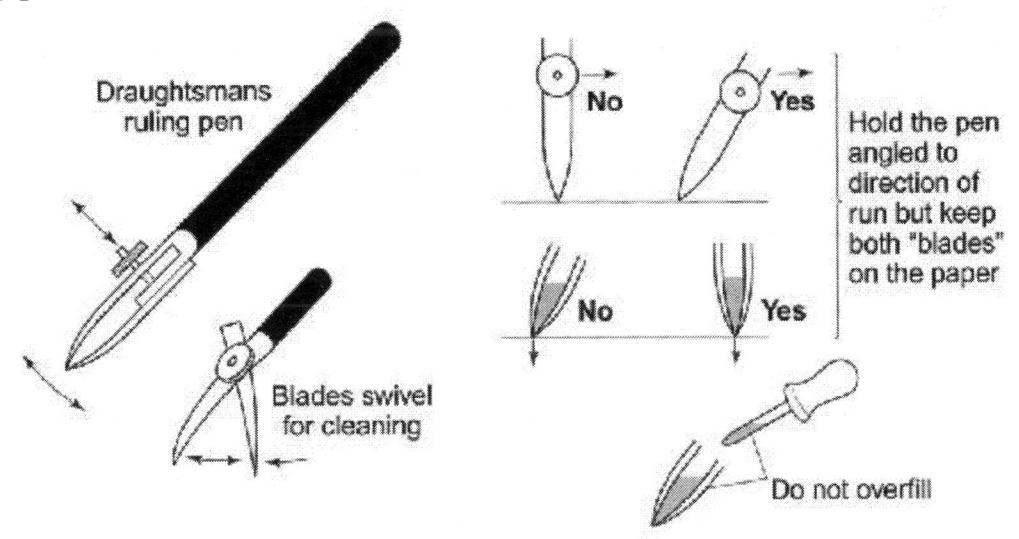

Using a draughtsman's ruling pen

For drawing lines, I use coloured acrylic inks which are fade-proof and which I water down to keep the lines subtle. A draughtsman's ruling pen (the pen usually found wit h sets of instruments) is a pair of pointed sprung "blades" that meet at the point and are adjusted by a knurled knob to set the width of line. You require the "deluxe" version that has a moveable lower "blade" to ensure you keep the pen clean. The pen is charged with a pipette or dropper that comes with the bottle of ink.

Deciding on the position of the lines is easy. For an even mount (same width all round), reverse the mount board (placed on card off-cut) and draw a line from the corner of the board to the corner of the aperture. Do this very accurately. Repeat for all four corners. Taking your dividers, open to the width of the first line from the aperture (if you have got "locking" or threaded dividers, all the better). Place this on the line, one point on the corner, the other where the first mark is to go. Push the pin through the card at this point to create a microscopic, barely visible hole on the face.

Washline mounts

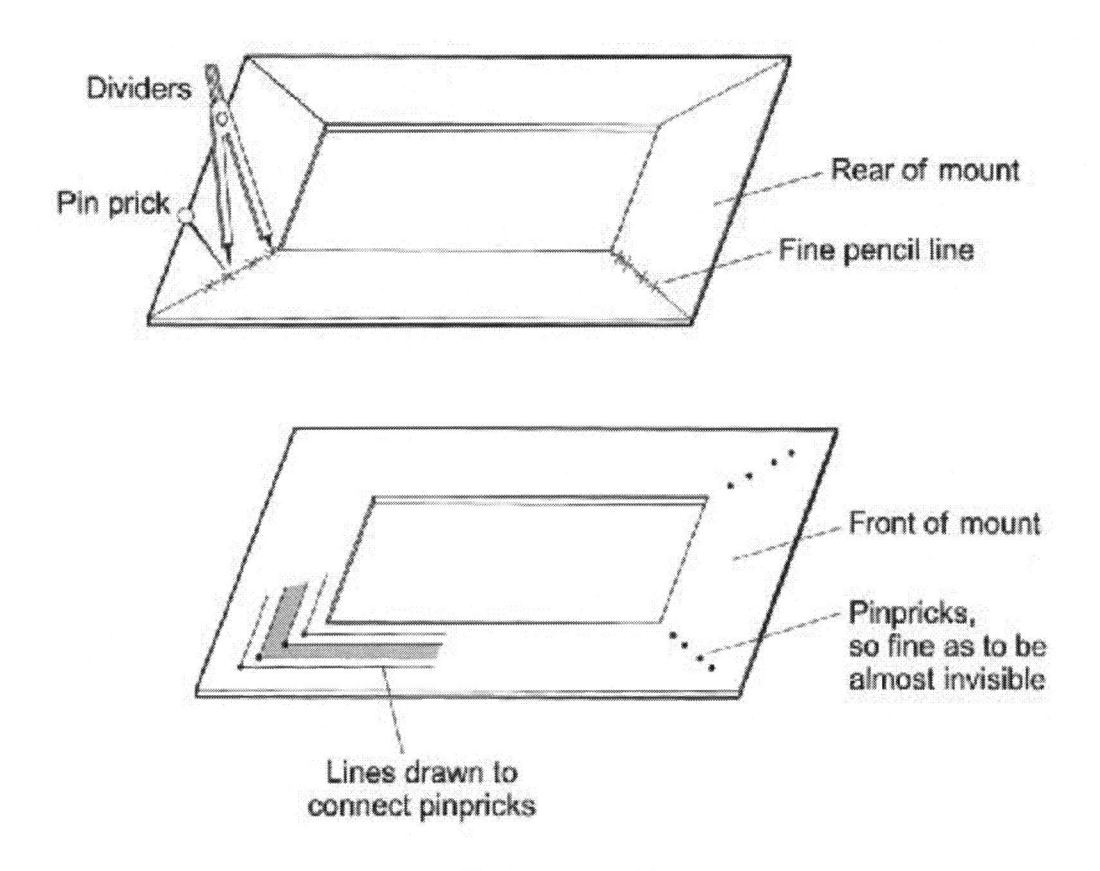

Repeat this on the other 3 corners, then readjust the point dividers to the next s pace you require. Place one point on the first mark then pierce the card and repeat on the other 3 sides.

Repeat the process until you have all points marked out then turn the mount board over and connect the dots (pin pricks) with your lining pen.

There is a small patent plastic insert that you can use to establish your points on the corner but I st ill use my old method as I am then sure I will have a wash line that corresponds to the cut out of the mount.

To draw the wash line, line up the straight edge with two adjacent pinholes. Then place the charged pen on the card against the straight edge and in ONE movement draw the line holding the pen slightly off the vertical while at the same time keeping both tips of the nib in contact with the card. Don't overload the pen with ink or gravity will blob the ink. Move positively and do not hesitate! Repeat on all four sides of he card and for as many lines as you think will compliment the picture.

Having drawn the lines and allowed them to dry, apply a wash between two of the lines using a fine brush, usually a pointed brush (size 4). Start at a corner with a neat line following the mitre line then in a careful continuous movement paint the colour between the lines around the mount. (not over them or your line will vary in colour intensity). Do not go back on yourself and do not stop until you can stop right against (and not over) your start point. Leave to dry.

The colour wash should be the same ink you use to draw the lines only watered down until its a thin tint of the original. You can, and I often do, use artist water-colour (from an artist sketch box with pans) to get the colour and effect I want. Practise will get you perfect wash lines and here I stress they must be perfect! Nothing looks more amateurish than badly executed lining work!

WASHLINE MOUNT

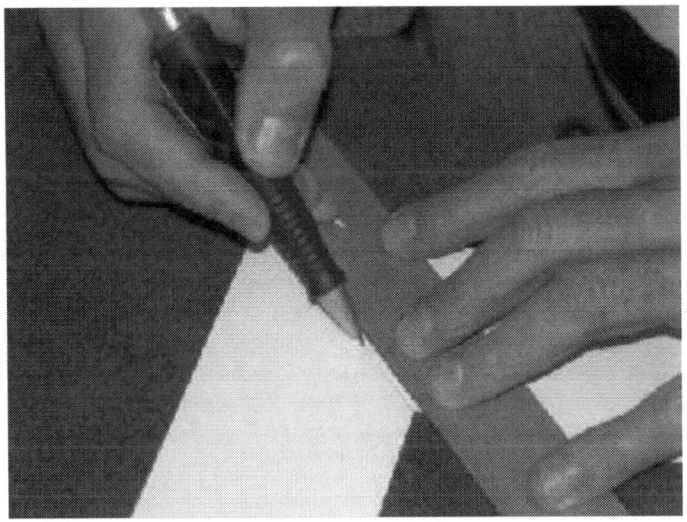

1. Draw line from inner corner to outer corner of mount, repeat for each corner

2. Shows diagonal lines on corners.

3. Use divides to establish line positions.

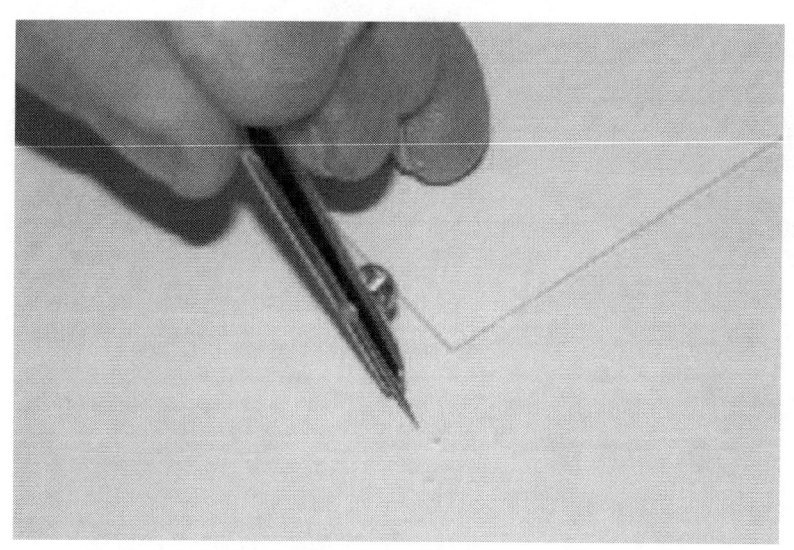

4. Use as fine a needle as possible to 'prick' mount board to establish points of reference on face of mount.

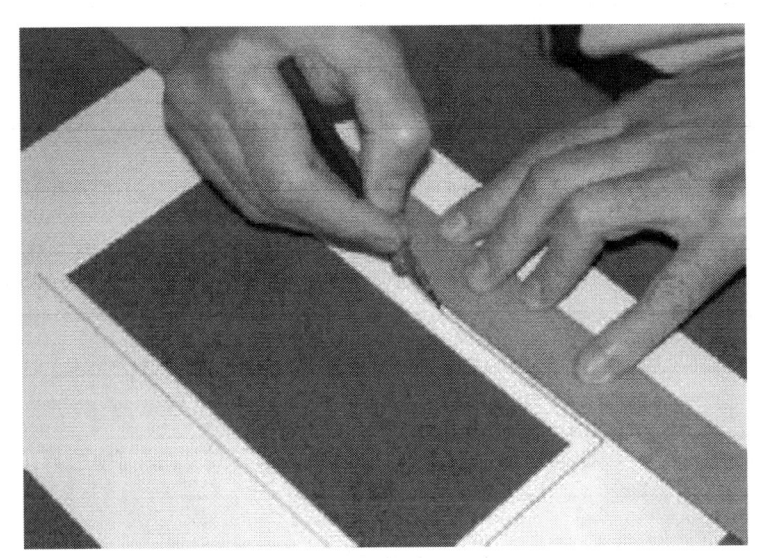

6 & 7 Carefully draw your lines from point (pin prick) to point (pin prick)

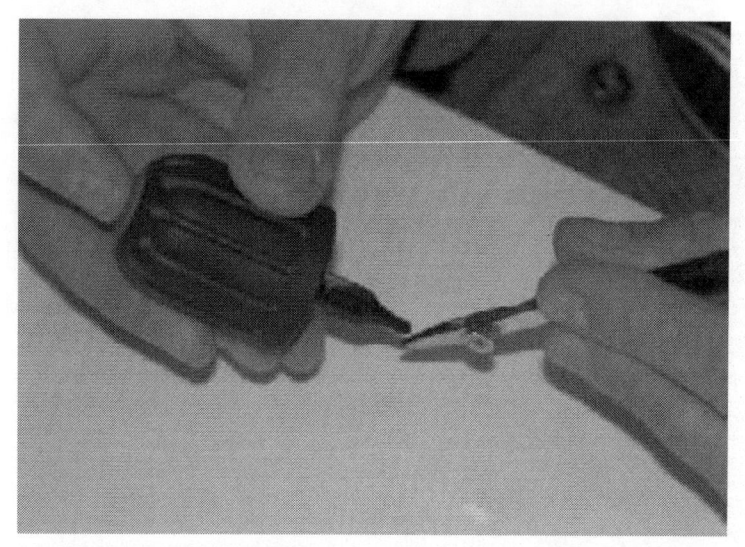

5. Charge the lining pen (over a piece of scrap board). Draw short 'test' line to ensure good flow.

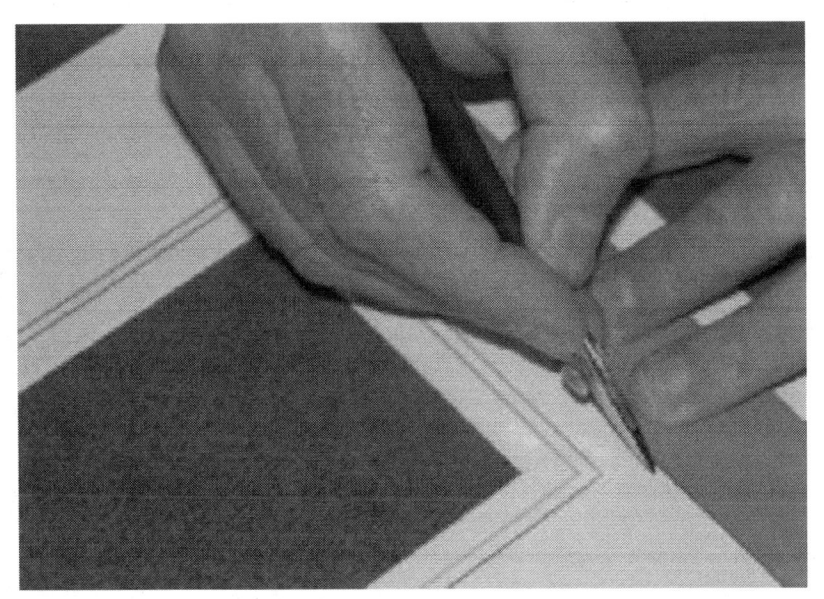

6 &7. Carefully draw your lines from point (pin prick) to point (pin prick)

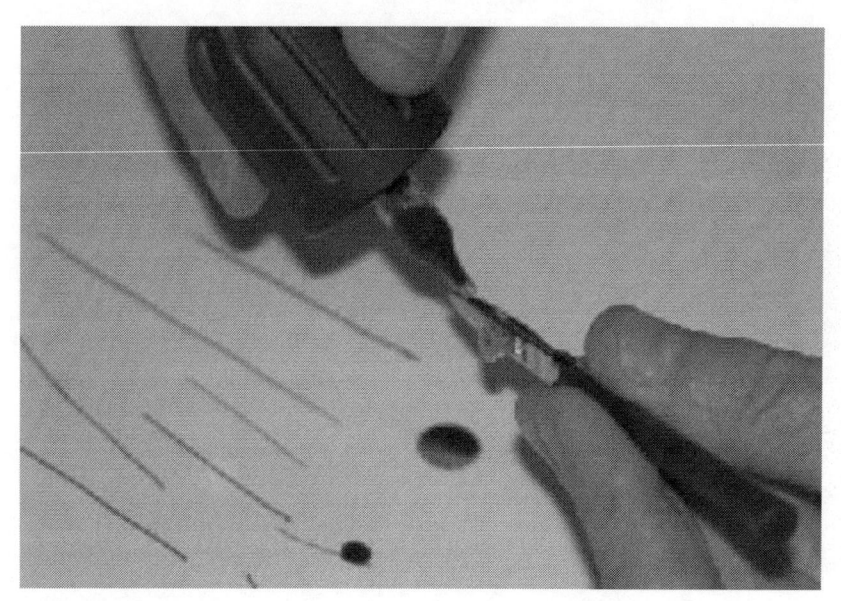

8. Carefully charge pen between EACH line

9. Draw the final line and allow to dry.

10. The lines ready for their wash.

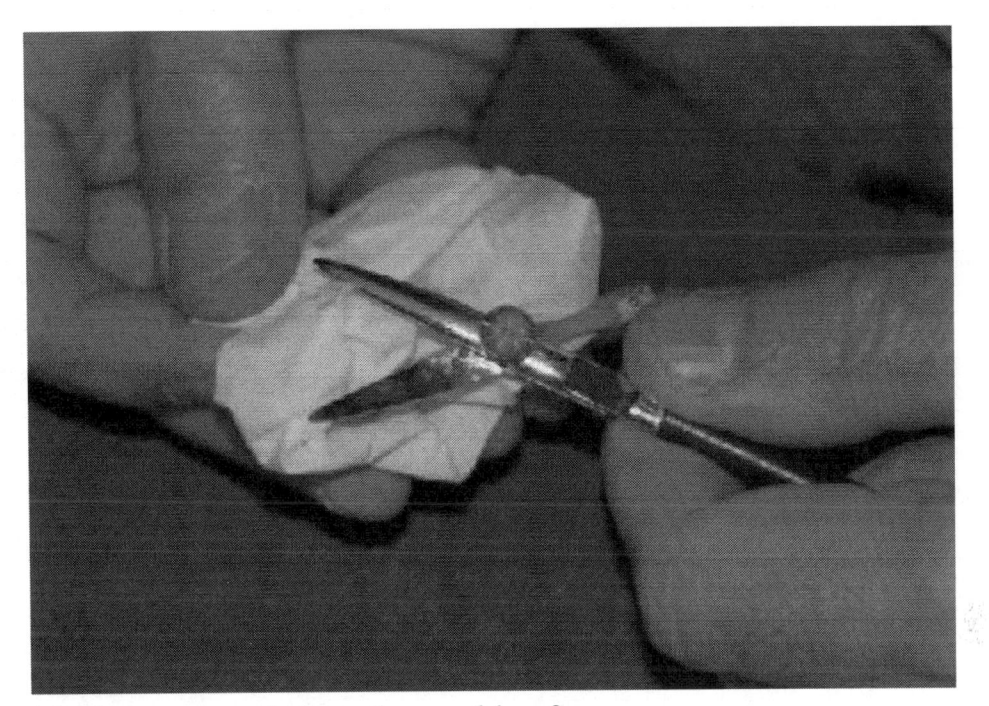

11. Open pen and clean thoroughly after use.

12

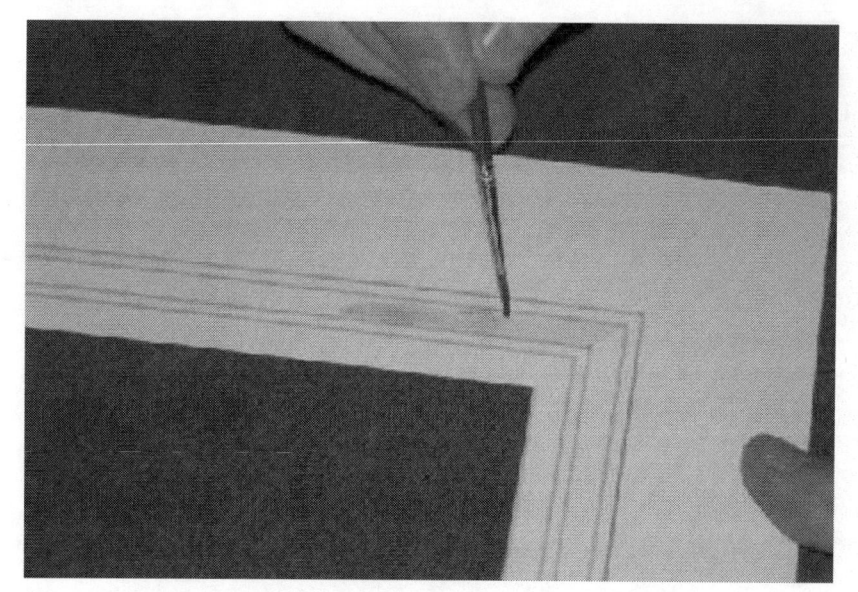

13

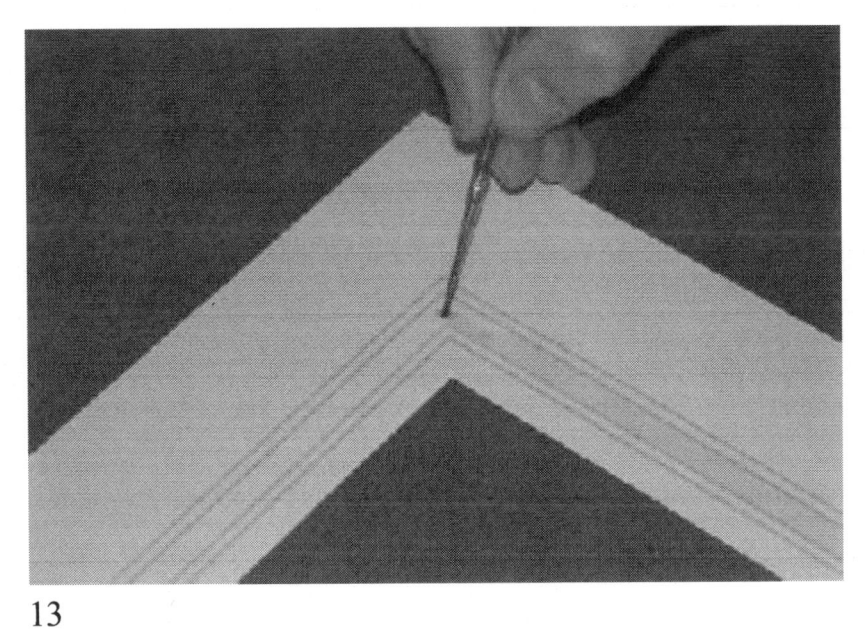

14

15. Use the same coloured ink or watercolour greatly watered down for the wash.
Start in a corner, working swiftly right around without going back on yourself until
you return to the first corner. Bring the wash up to this point without crossing the
first wash - great care and accuracy is the secret.

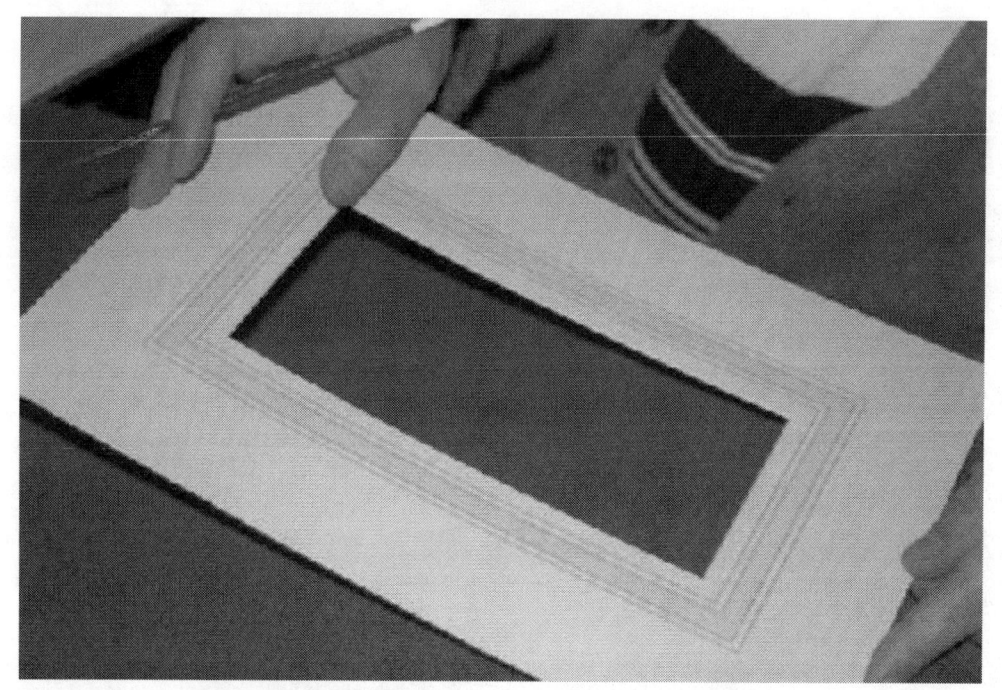

16. The washline mount.

You can combine your wash line with multiple mounts or gold lining using either pens or leaf. You will find yourself forever studying frames for ideas. Great sources of inspiration are very old frames round pictures brought in for re-framing. The old framers achieved wonderful effects with very little limited materials.

Oval Mounts

Oval mounts are virtually impossible to cut without some k ind of machine from the big micrometer thread oval cutters that cut both card and glass, to the simple arm on an offset base that describes an oval which is your best solution until you want to splash out on a full size cutting machine (the machine I possess has a fitting for a drawing pen to produce oval wash lines - I've never tried to wash line an oval mount by hand!). Be very accurate when cutting your oval mount and assembling it into the frame as inaccuracies shout out at you!

Mount cutting and mount preparation are probably the most time consuming part of the frame making process. I have a basic range of mount effects that I know I can execute quickly, neatly and effectively to ensure I do not become bogged down on any individual frame. Time is money so if a customer wants intricate and lavish work, you should charge for it.

THREE DIMENSIONAL OBJECTS, BOX FRAMES, DISPLAY CASES

From time to time you will get 3D objects to frame, the most common being medals and coins.

The coins are best framed in mount board individually cut to take the coins. I do this by placing the coin on the mount board tracing it faintly in pencil and carefully cutting out the disc with a scalpel. There is a special cutter for this purpose, a compass like device holding a blade which you rotate through the card. It works very well.

Medals are often mounted on velvet or silk glued onto a backing. The medals are then fixed on a bar. Once again don't damage the ribbons when you frame medals give them an expansive frame. Close framed, they look insignificant! The framing equipment you use is also ideal for making display cases of all descriptions. You will find that your local builders' merchant carries various wood mouldings for the carpentry trade. These you can adapt easily to framing or making display cases along with the various prepared timber lengths - always use the best quality kiln dried! Your mitre guillotine will cut angles other than 45 degrees, in fact it will cut any angle up to 90 degrees. Remember that if you make frames or cases that require any work with power tools, routers or saws, they create huge dust problems for your other framing activities and I would always recommend a separate "dusty" work area or room.

As with all aspects of framing, the wholesalers now carry a range of box framing devices, extensions to moulding, spacing bars. Use them by all means, but do not buy all sorts of patent aids when you start framing: they are a drain on resources and can be gradually added to your equipment as you find you have need of them.

TAPESTRIES & EMBROIDERIES

Tapestries

The system I use for stretching tapestries, I first devised 25 years ago and it has never failed me. In recent years I have seen tapestries I stretched and framed then and they are still perfect,. So I can say with certainty that the following method has withstood the test of time.

First measure the tapestry exactly then add 3mm to each side length. Then make the stretch frame. This comprises a wood frame on a card board sheet. I carry ramin battens or planks in the following sizes: 40 x 5mm (1½ x ¼in.) for small, 50 x 5mm (2 x ¼in.) for medium and 64 x 5mm (2.½ x .¼in.) for large tapestries.

Cut your wood batten to the size you have measured - that's the outer side of the frame - glue and clamp the mitres, spread glue on one face of the wood frame (I use PVA wood glue) and place on top of an off-cut sheet of mount board. Place the whole assembly under weights to dry overnight.

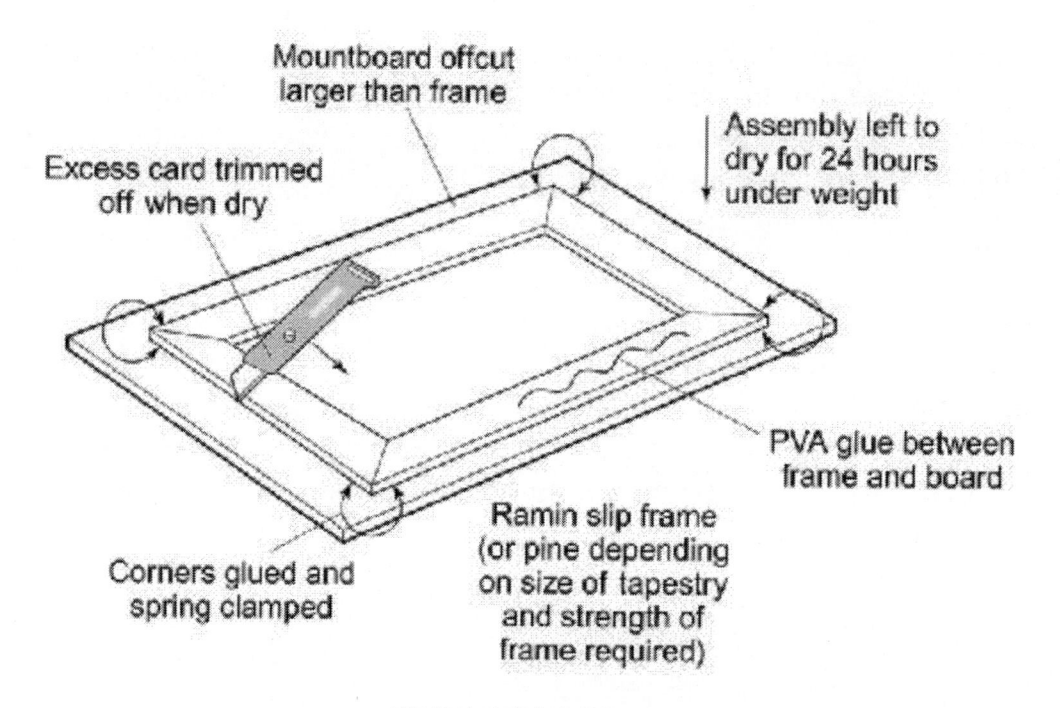

Tapestry stretcher frame

Once the frame is dry, trim the card to the frame edge with a Stanley knife then stretch on the tapestry. Simply start at one corner and hold and staple (using a stationery staple gun with 6mm staples - they are easier to remove if necessary) making sure that the staples are in the wood not the card.

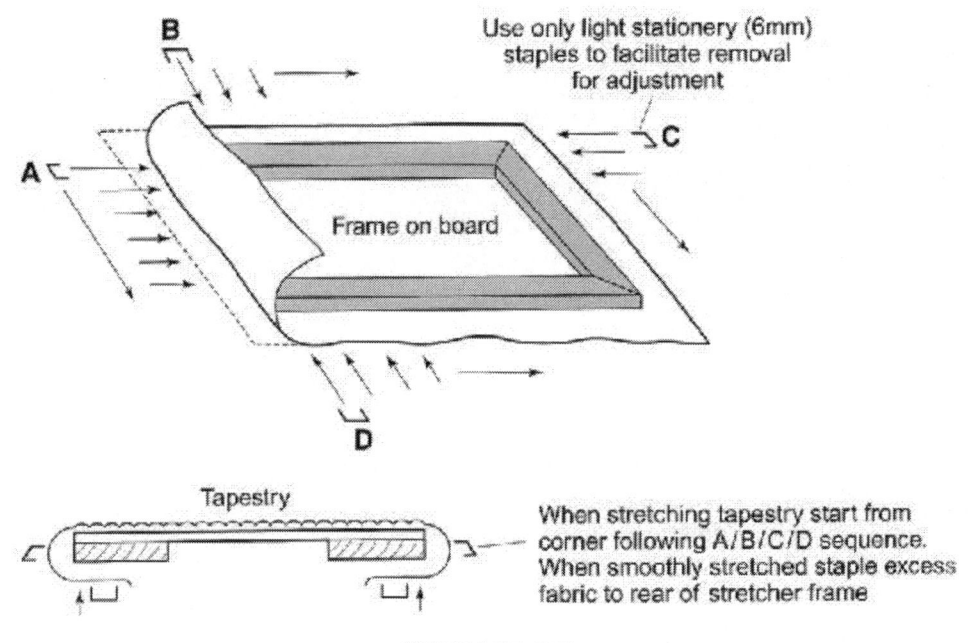

Use only light stationery (6mm) staples to facilitate removal for adjustment

When stretching tapestry start from corner following A/B/C/D sequence. When smoothly stretched staple excess fabric to rear of stretcher frame

Stretching tapestry

Work down the length and width making sure you are dead straight and pulling the tapestry into position. Follow with the remaining two sides. Here you will have to pull much harder to align the tapestry. The more distorted the customer has made the tapestry, the bigger the battle! If the tapestry is very badly distorted, thicken the wood on the stretcher to take the strain. The result should be a perfectly flat tapestry, held with all the stitches straight. Again, practise makes perfect. I invariably box frame my tapestries so that the "fluffiness" of the surface is not crushed by the glass. The inner frame I usually paint to match the predominant tapestry colour.

Box-framed tapestry

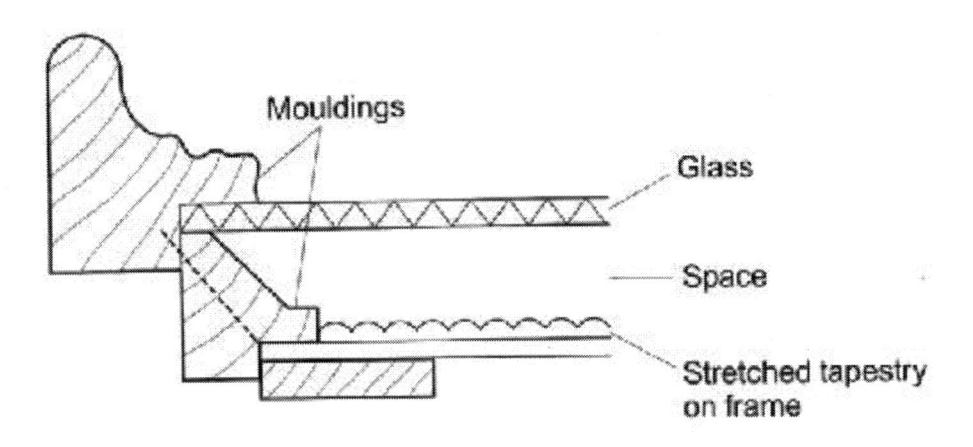

There is only one potential problem with this method and that is corrosion of the staples damaging the fabric. So as an added precaution I have always put a minute dab of copy dex over the staples to keep them moisture free - 25 year old tapestries still have bright metal staples. Copydex is the only glue apart from resin W wood adhesive (PVA) that I keep in the workshop. A latex based glue it is totally inert once cured. (Incidentally if you are pruning trees, paint it on the cut ends to seal the wound!)

STRETCHING A TAPESTRY

1. The frame, wood strip/batten is glued to mount board for extra strength

2. Pull/fold round frame

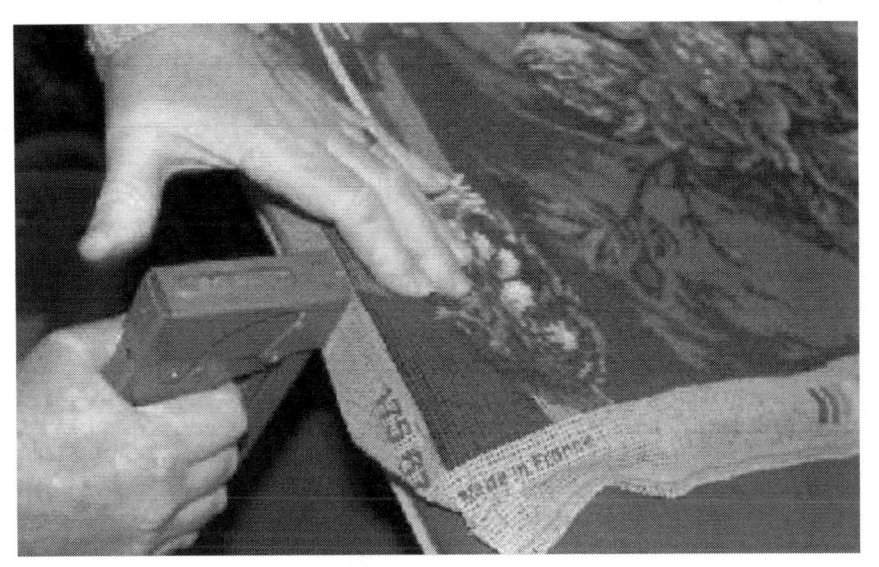

3. Start stapling from corner.

4.....

& 5. Continue pulling, aligning and stapling along side until all edges are fixed and tapestry is flat, straight and taut.

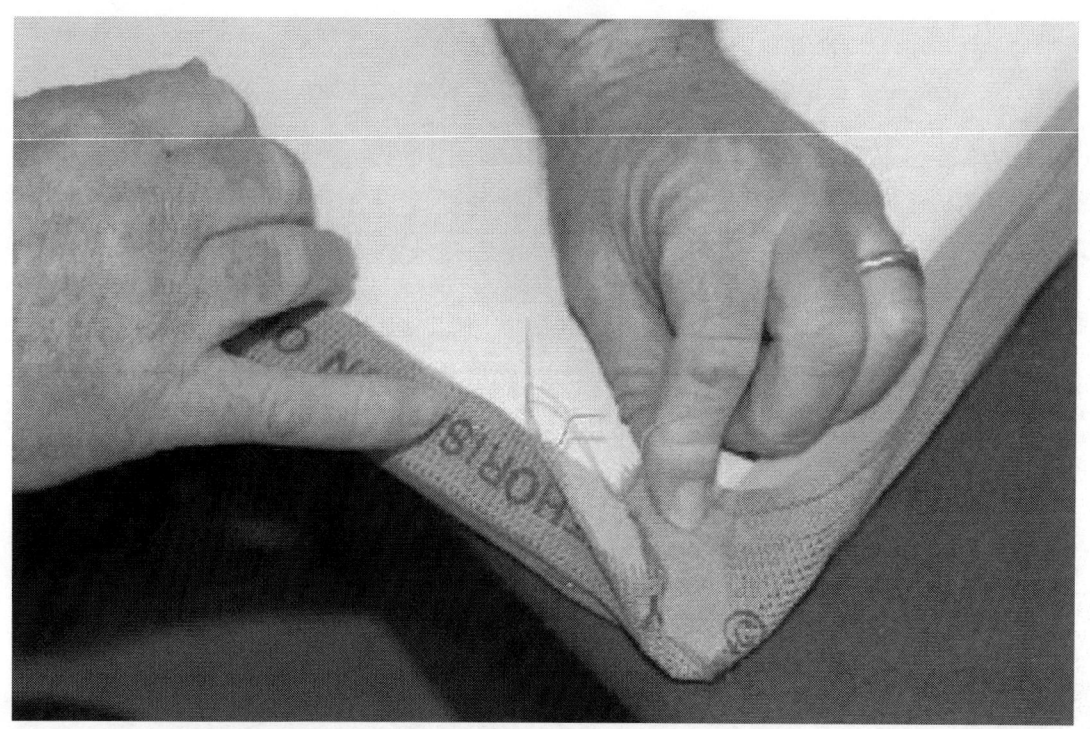

6, 7, 8, 9, 10. Fold and staple the corners.

7.

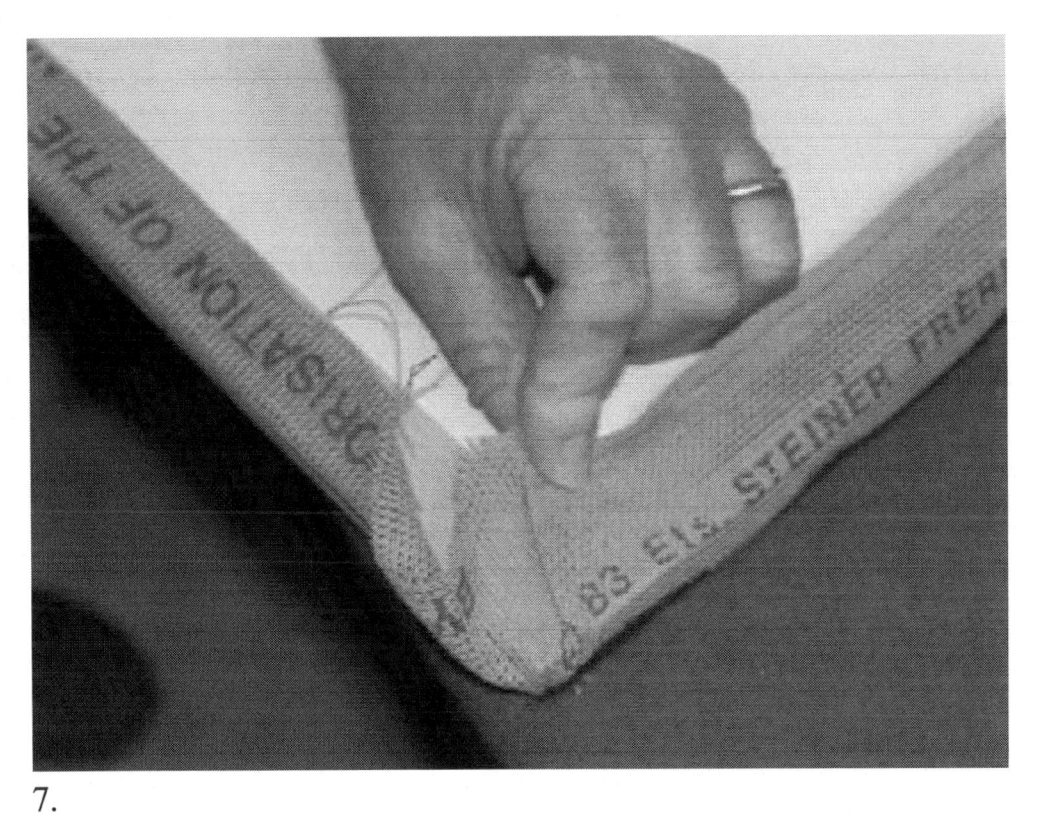

8.

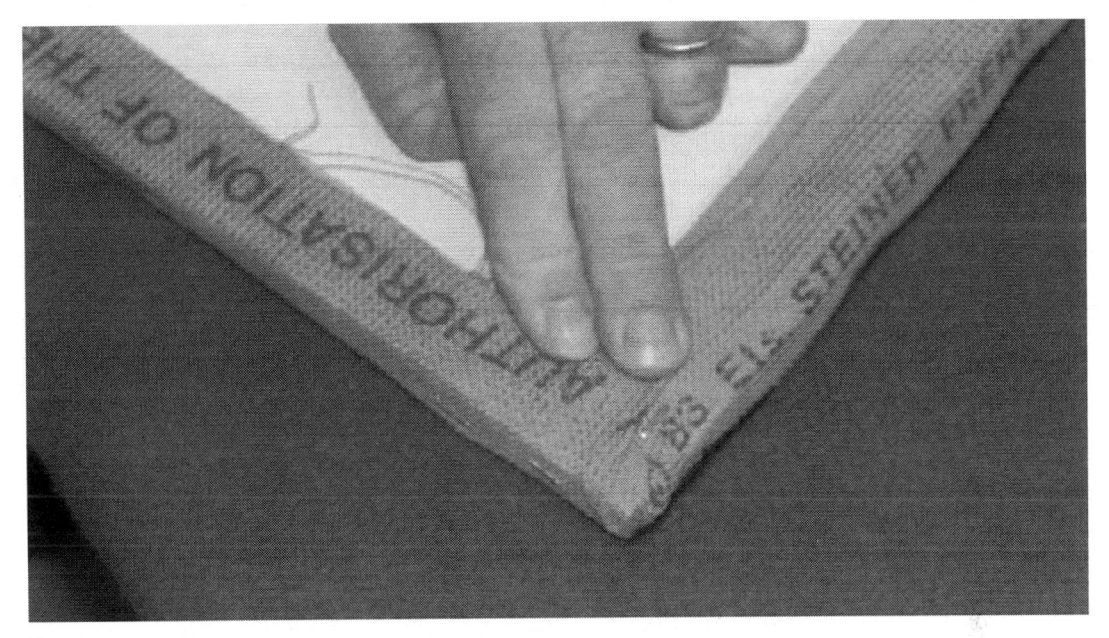

9.

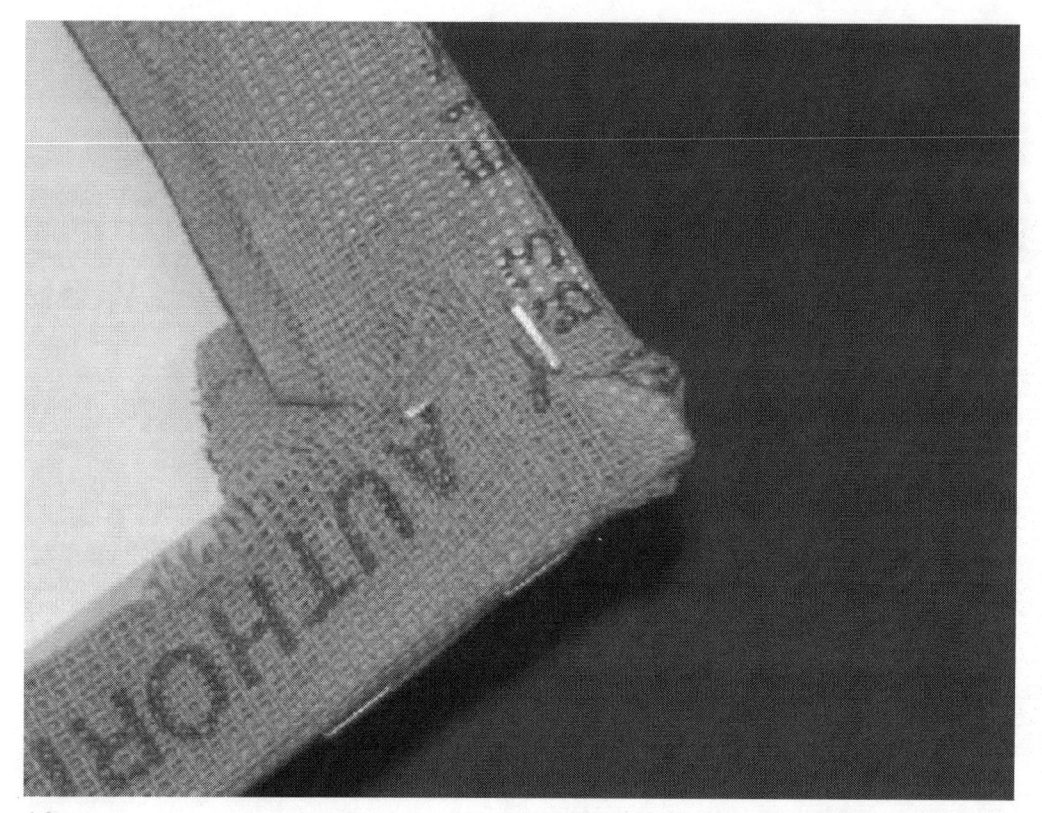

10.

11. The stretched tapestry ready to be framed.

Cross stitch & Needle Point

For cross stitch and needle point, I cut a thin white (acid free) card and punch the edges of the card with a "ring binding" punch - allowing plenty of space for the picture. The fixings are covered by the mount or slip. The needle point is then stitched onto the card.

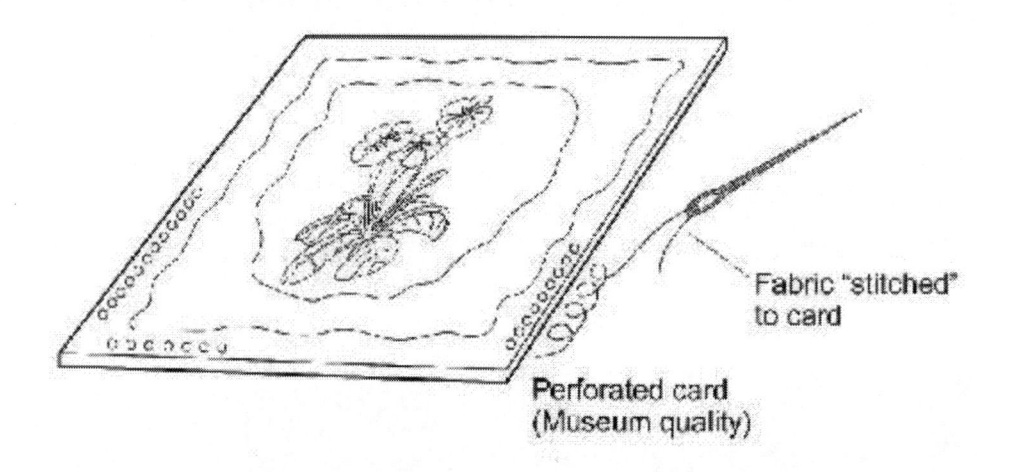

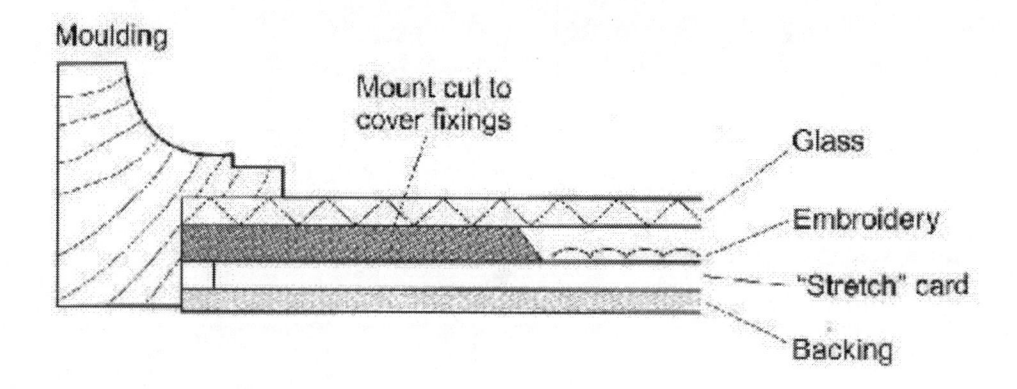

Fabric "stitched" to card

Perforated card (Museum quality)

Moulding

Mount cut to cover fixings

Glass

Embroidery

"Stretch" card

Backing

The second method is to take a card (acid free) and put double sided tape on the rear of the card and bring the fabric round to stick it on the rear, pulling the face taunt. Once positioned and held, use masking tape to lock down the edges. If you use this method, go to the extreme edge of the fabric so that any damage the glues in the tapes inflict can be removed without detriment to the artwork.

The third method is to 'lace' the cross stitch onto the card by folding the ends of the fabric round the card then lacing up the sides.

Card and double-sided tape

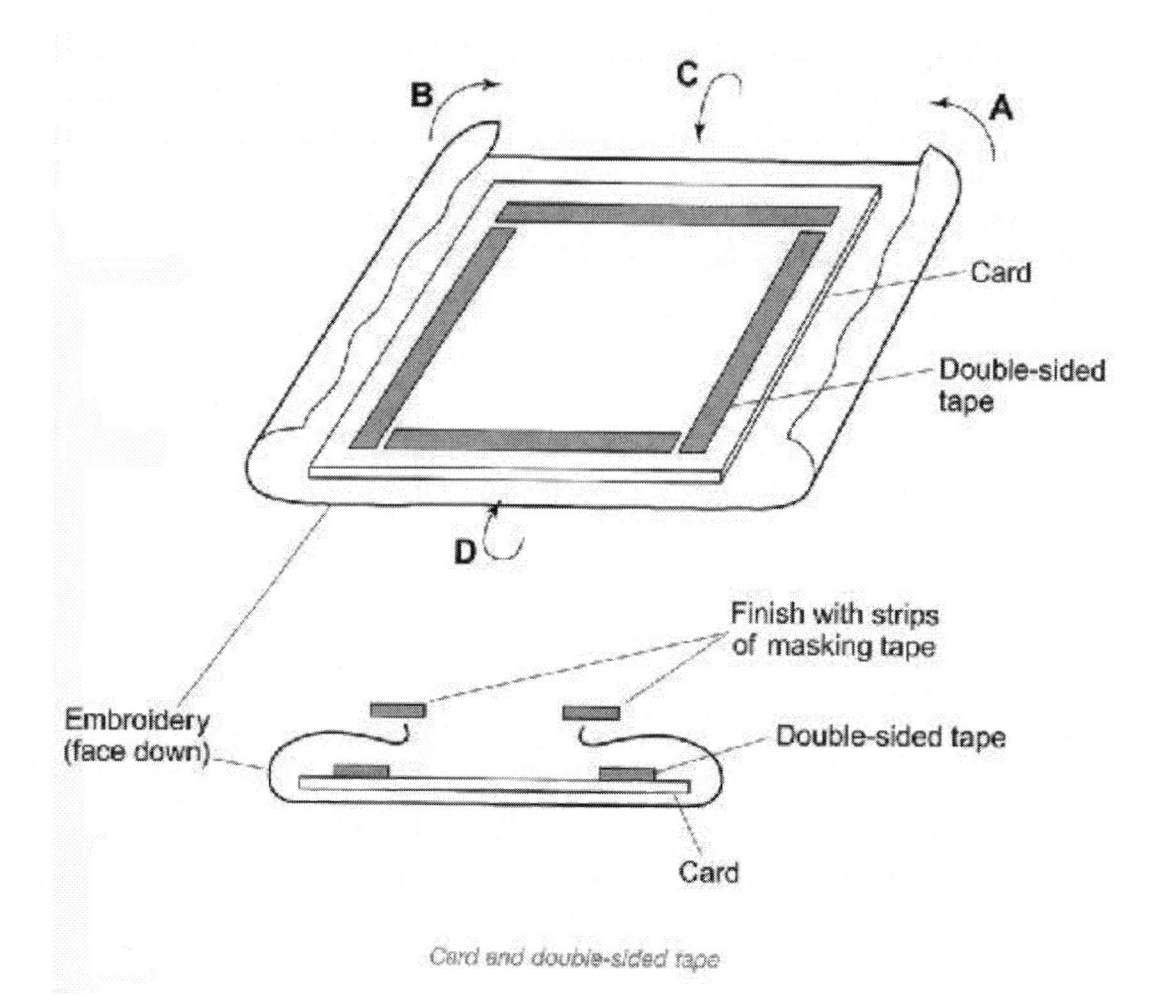

When you make a box frame using the battens, first cut the frame whilst at the same time cut the battens. Make the frame up and when dry, clean and fit the glass, then fit the 4 battens to form the box . Pin and glue to the rear of the rebate. Having fitted this, cut 4 pieces of identical width batten to fit to the outside of the boxing that is in the frame. It must be snug, exact fit. Glue and clamp it to the inner and in doing so, you will have formed a rebate to accommodate the backing board.

I once had a customer with a very special embroidery who wanted the work suspended in a frame with no fixings. My first reaction was "how?", the second, "impossible" but he insisted so I asked him to go away and put two "loops" (fold over and stitch the top and bottom) in the top and bottom of the piece, which he did. I then made a box frame using the 40mm (1.½in.) ramin battens with a turn button back. I drilled through the sides of the "box" and inserted two 12mm (.5in.) pieces of dowel. The fabric was then hung top and bottom on the dowel and the back closed and taped.

STRETCHING A CROSS STITCH

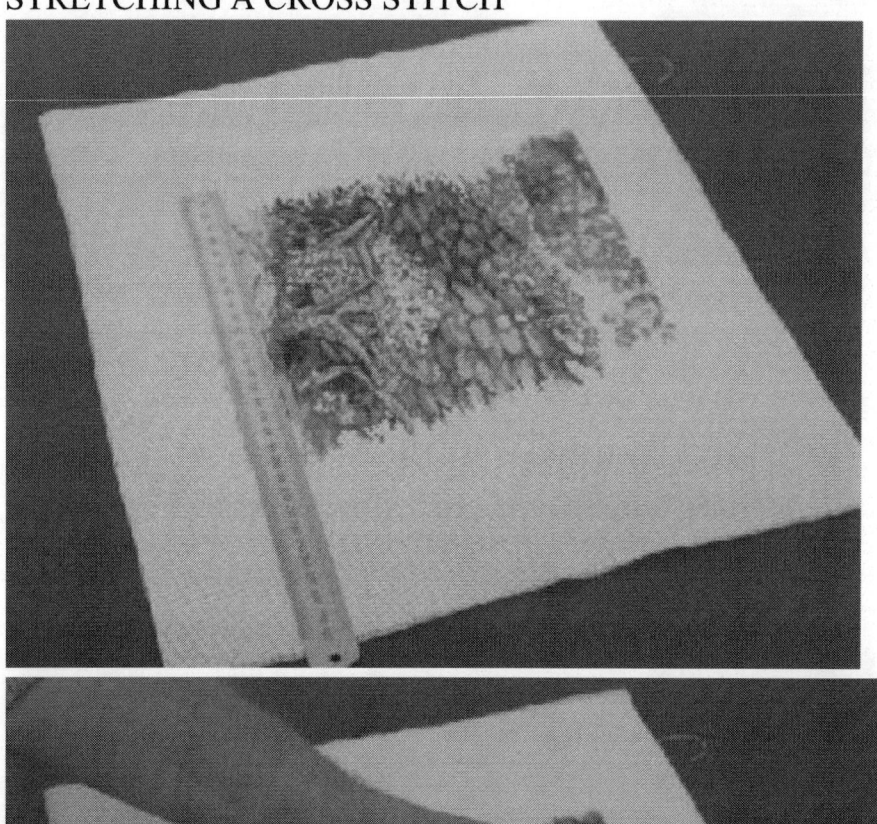

1 & 2. Measure artwork.

3.& 4. Cut backing board to size.

4.

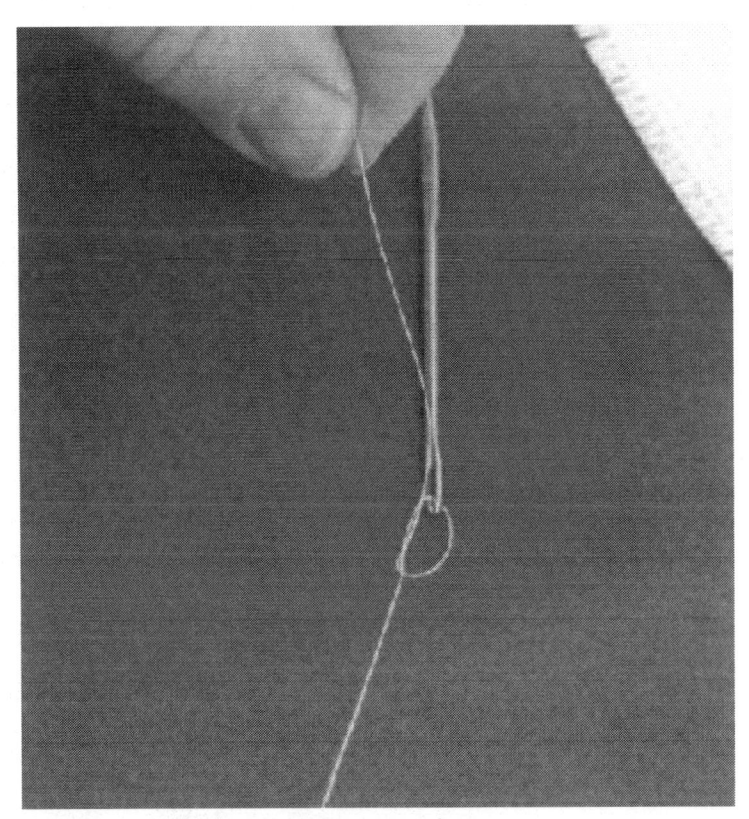

5. Knot cotton thread onto needle.
Leave bobbin loose on floor or bench so you can pull the thread as you need it.

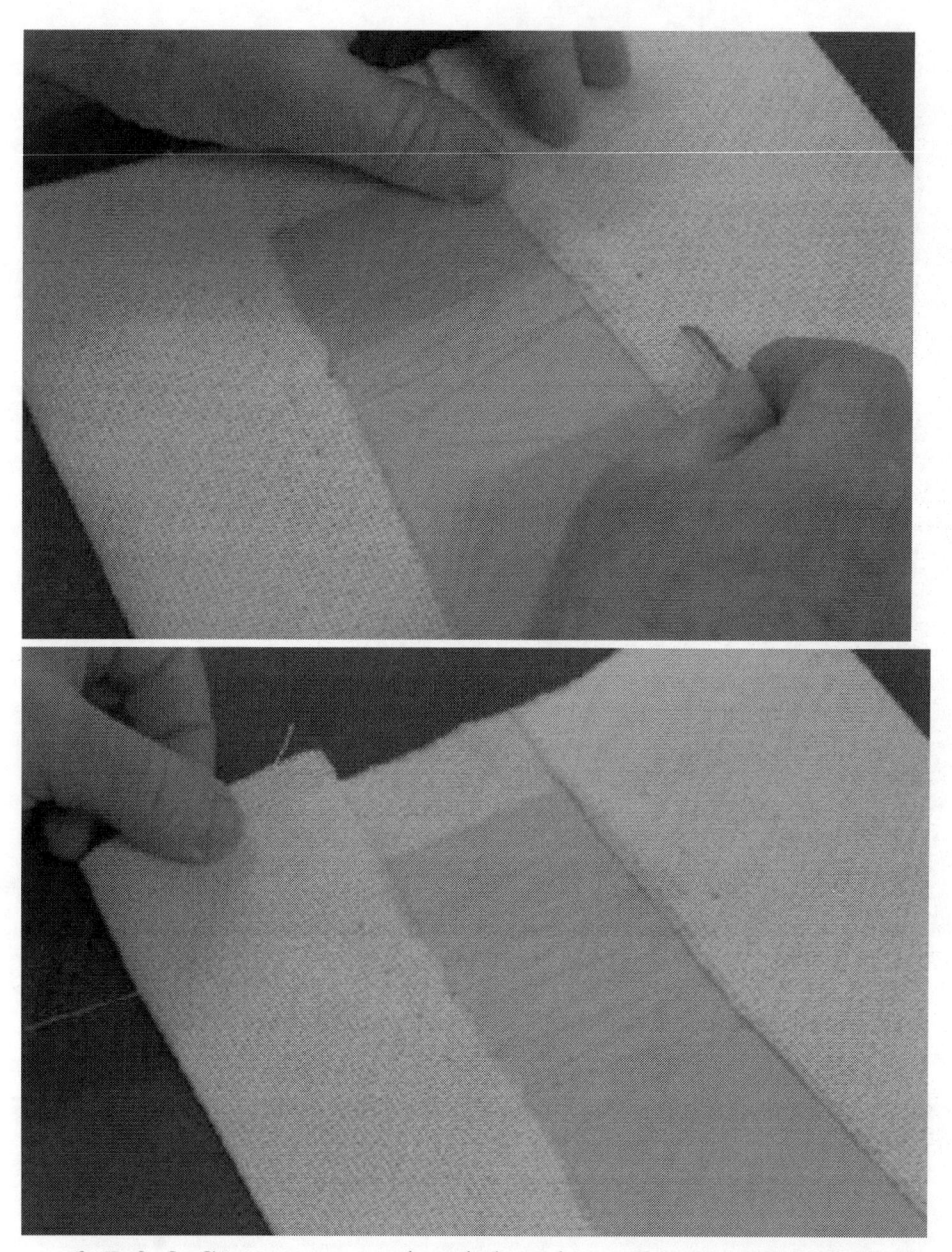

6, 7 & 8. Start at one end and 'bootlace' the thread through the fabric keeping straight and well from the edge.

6.

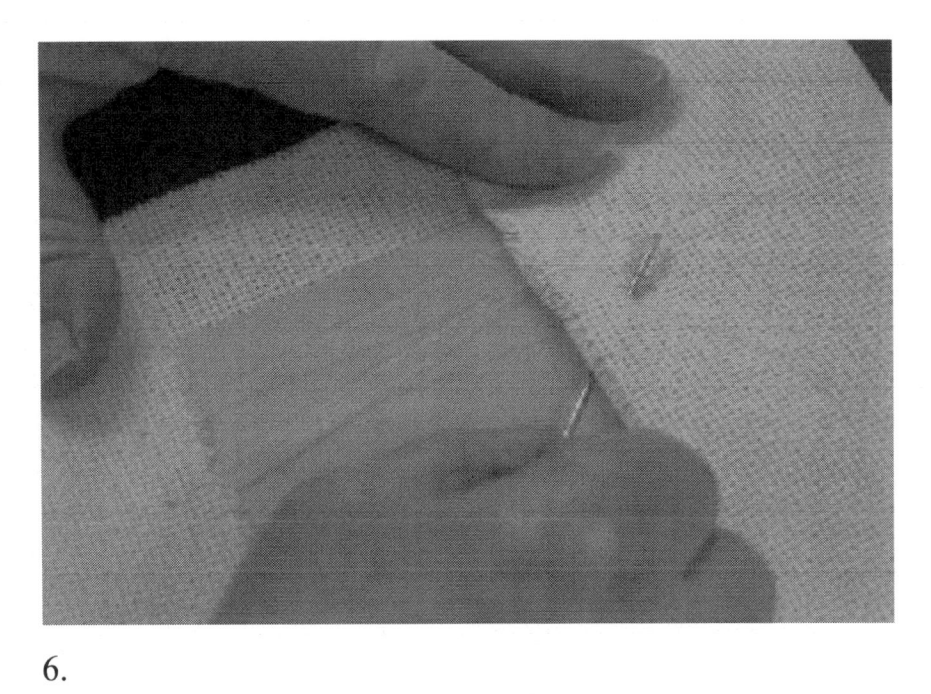

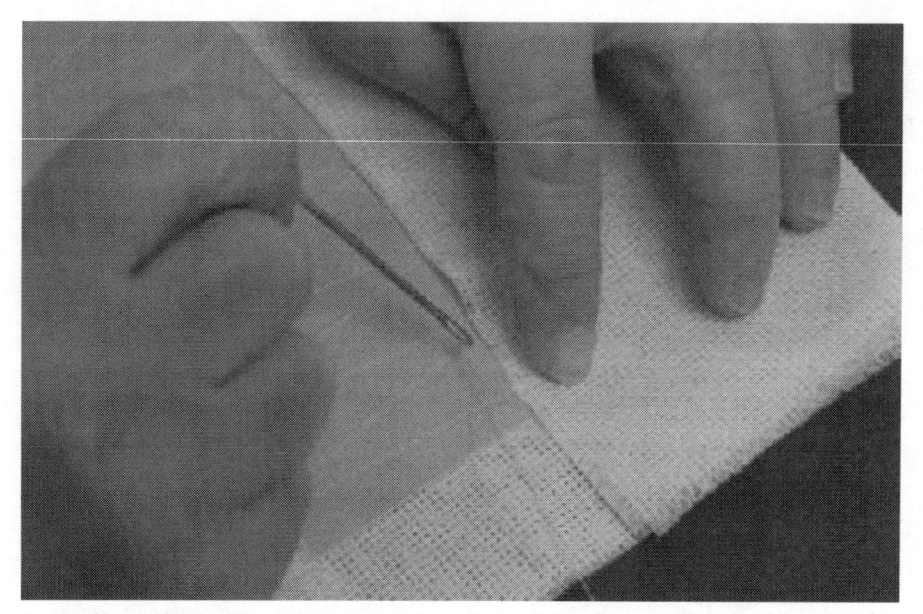

9. Pull and tension the thread so it holds the artwork flat, firm and straight on the backing board, then tie off the thread.

10. Carefully fold corner.

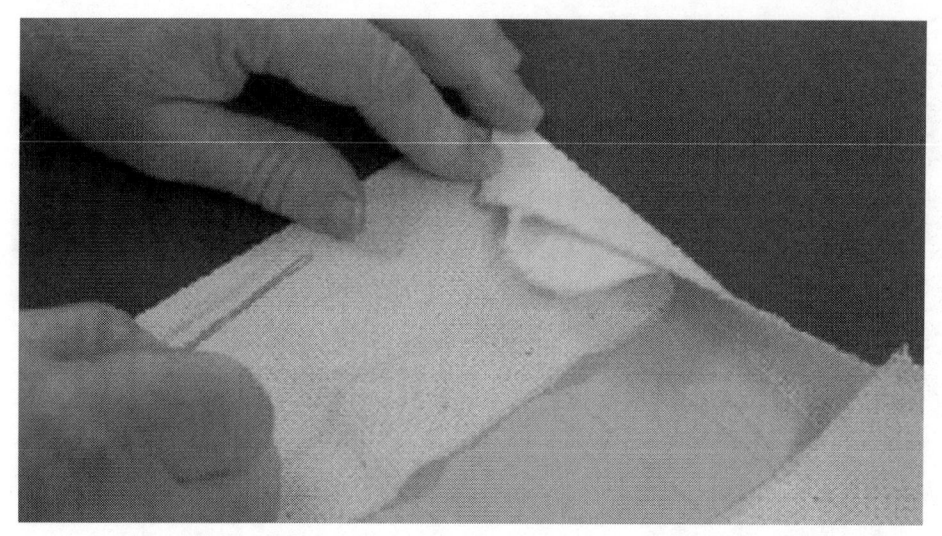

11, & 12. Repeat the boot lacing in opposite direction. Pull taut.

12.

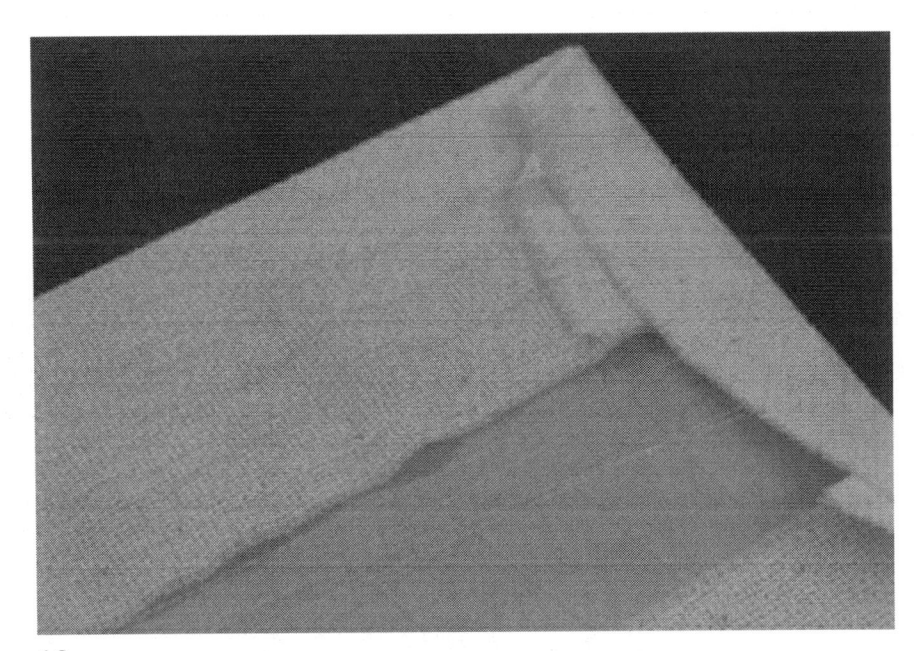

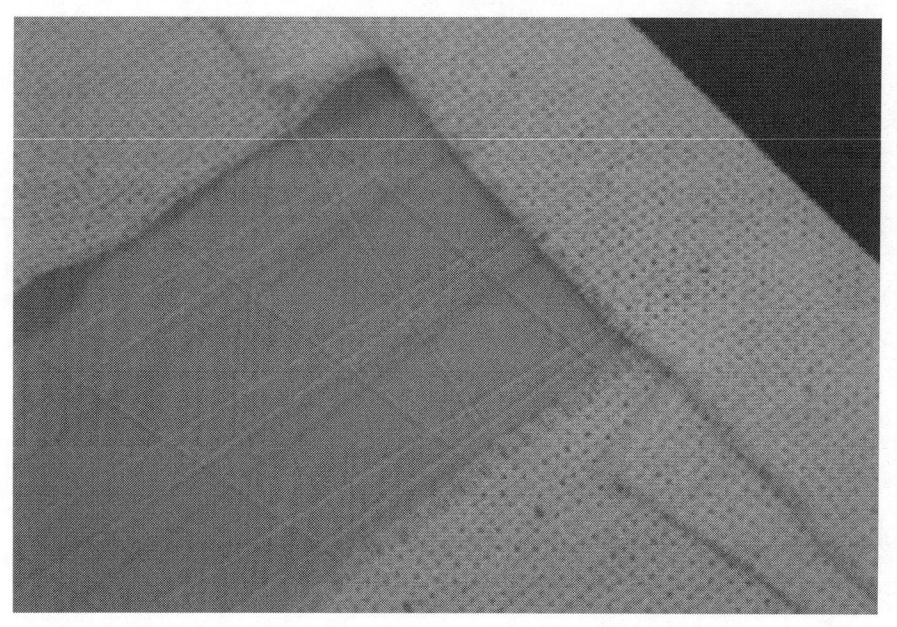

13. Detail showing lacing in both directions holding al four edges firmly.

14. The stretched cross stitch ready to be framed.

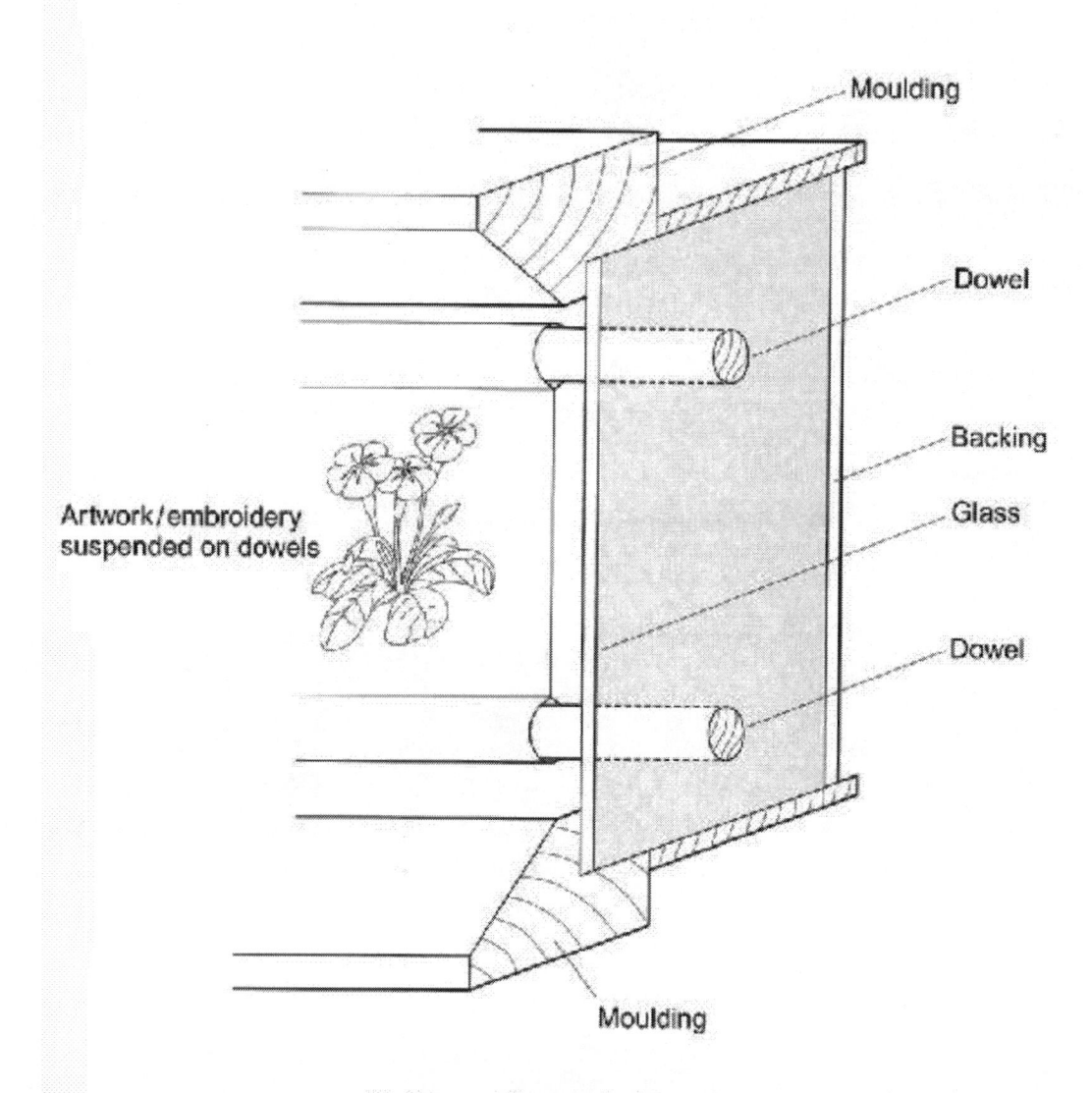

Box frame with suspended artwork

When I first knew my wife, I bought her some very expensive, exquisite lace handkerchiefs whilst I was on the continent. Unbeknown to me, she had them framed. I did not think anymore of this until we moved house and I was packing the framed lace when I noticed a yellow stain on each of the handkerchiefs. I took the frame to the workshop and opened it up to discover the framer had stuck the handkerchiefs down with some sort of glue or double sided tape that had rapidly attacked the cloth leaving brittle yellow patches. Needless to say the lace work was ruined and the result was a treasured sentimental item thrown away! The handkerchiefs should have been mounted with very fine stitches using matching cotton onto white museum board. If you have glues, beware! Think how to mount artwork with its long term good in mind. You are the expert; the customer trusts you and you have a responsibility to them.

Looking through various suppliers catalogues, there are numerous needlework stretching and mounting devices. Try them out till you find the system that suits you best.

Shadow Box

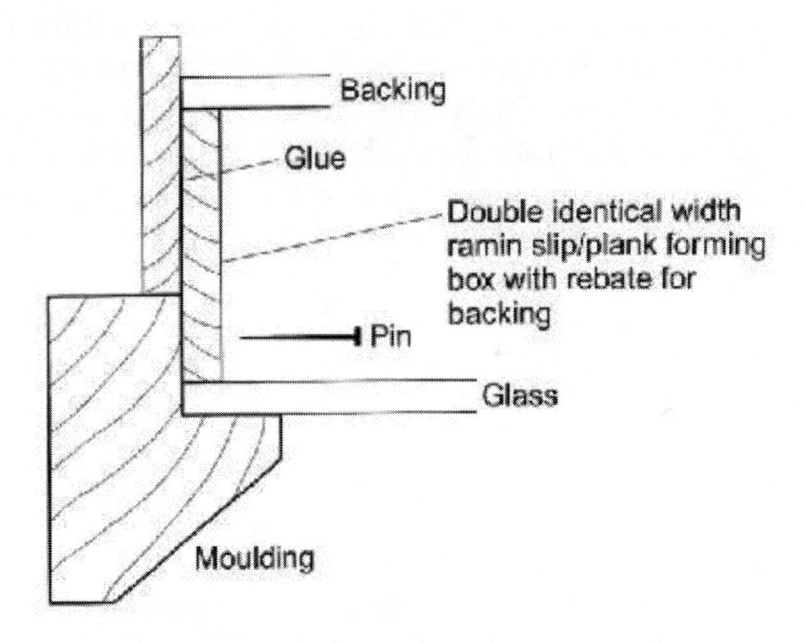

Forming a rebate to accommodate the backing board

STRETCHING CANVAS

You will either come across artists who want their canvas stretched, or, more commonly, a customer who has brought a painting on canvas which has been rolled for transport and needs to be remounted on a stretcher frame. Stretcher frames are sold in prefabricated lengths. The ends have a "tongue and slot" configuration that slot into one another and allow for a pair of wooden wedges per corner once the canvas is stretched onto the frame. It can be tensioned by tapping the wedges in to expand the corner joint.

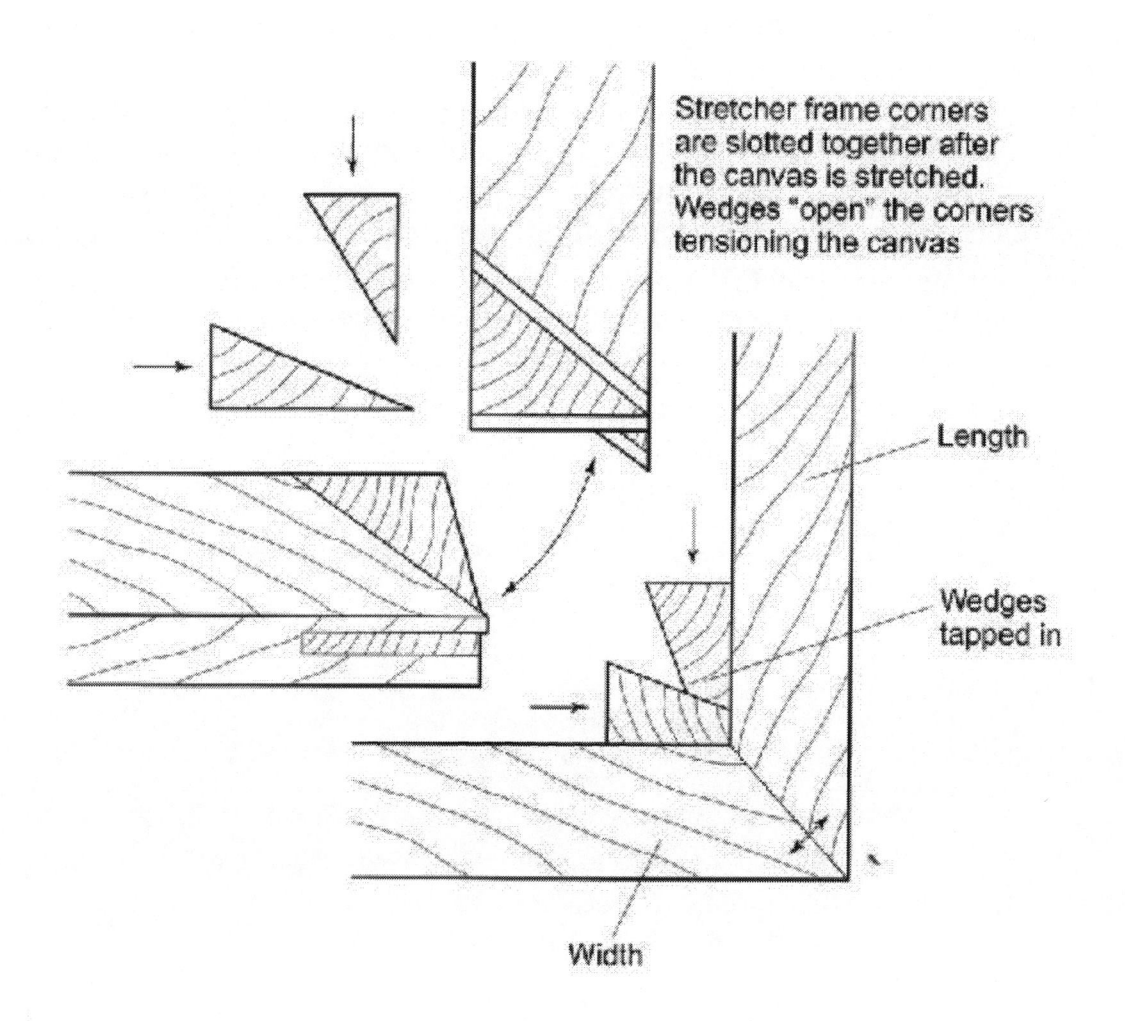

Stretcher frame corners are slotted together after the canvas is stretched. Wedges "open" the corners tensioning the canvas

Length

Wedges tapped in

Width

Stretcher-frame corners slotted together

To stretch a canvas, firstly fit the four sides of the stretch frame together and place on a bench. Using your set square, check that the frame is square for if it is not square you will have problems when it comes to the framing! Lay the canvas face down on the bench and place the stretcher frame on top. If it is a picture you are mounting, make sure you align the holes from its previous fixing to correspond to the stretch frame sides where you will be fixing. Once you are satisfied the canvas is accurately fixed, take the centre of the first edge (usually that facing you), fold the canvas up the side of the stretcher bar and pin either using the traditional "tack" or as I do, a 6mm stationery gun stapler. Then take the *opposite* bar pull the canvas taught over the edge using a pair of canvas pliers or your hands (depending on your grip), and staple. Repeat this on the other two sides.

Pulling canvas taut and stapling

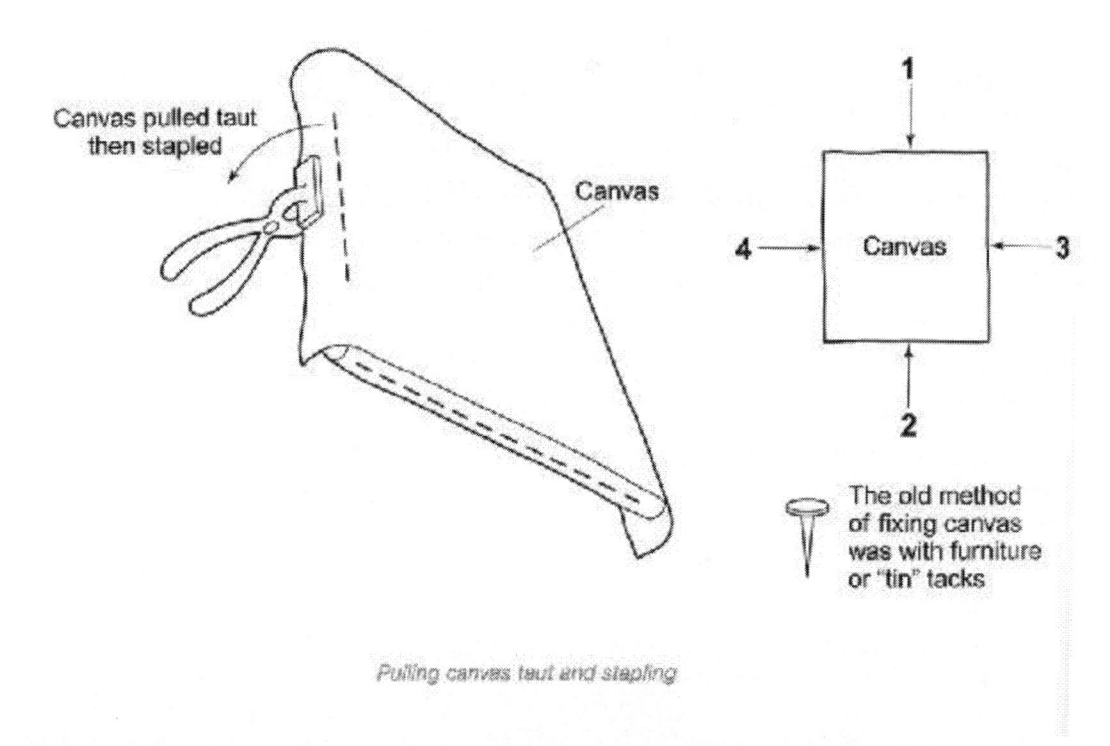

You will now have the canvas held on the stretcher at four points, one on each side. Start on one side and from the middle to the corner, stretch and staple the canvas until the entire side is stapled. Repeat this on the opposite side, pulling the canvas taut. Once done, repeat on the other two sides.

NB. You can use tacks instead of staples

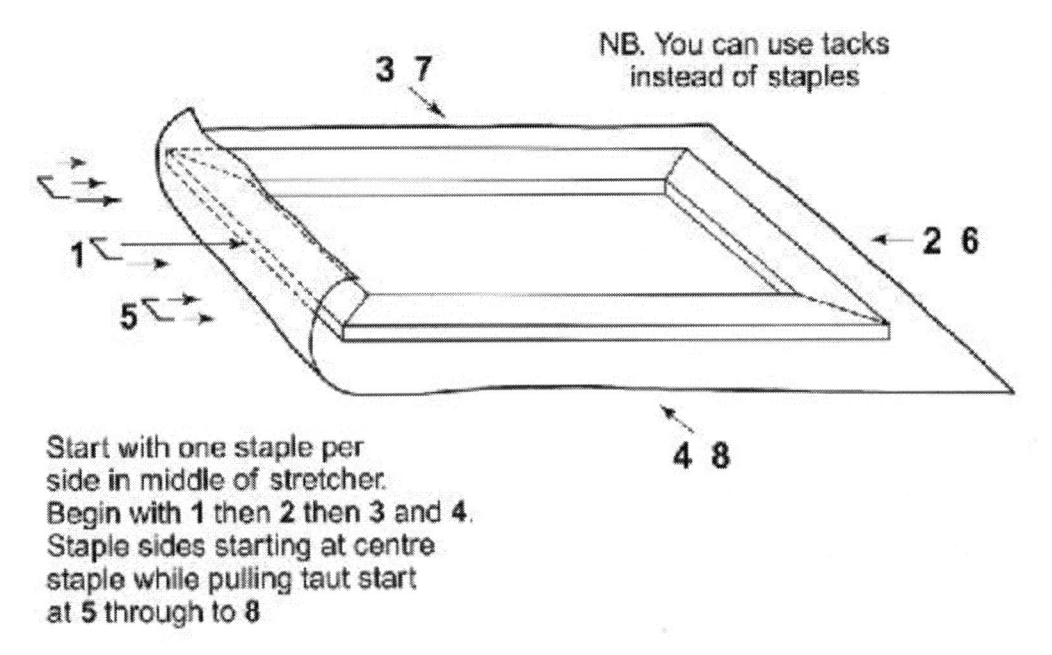

3 7

1

5

2 6

4 8

Start with one staple per
side in middle of stretcher.
Begin with **1** then **2** then **3** and **4**.
Staple sides starting at centre
staple while pulling taut start
at **5** through to **8**

Stapling or tacking

Once the canvas is stretched over the frame, lay it face down and fold the corners of the canvas one at a time. Pull it up over the frame, hold it down, take the two side flaps and pull these up and hold down and staple both to the back of the stretcher frame. Repeat on the other corners then staple the canvas all round on to the back of the stretcher. Once neatly fixed, insert the eight wedges and gently tap in to tension the canvas - it should be smooth, taut but not over-stretched to distortion. (NB: when stretching tapestries, you start at the corner but with a canvas, you start in the middle of each side.)

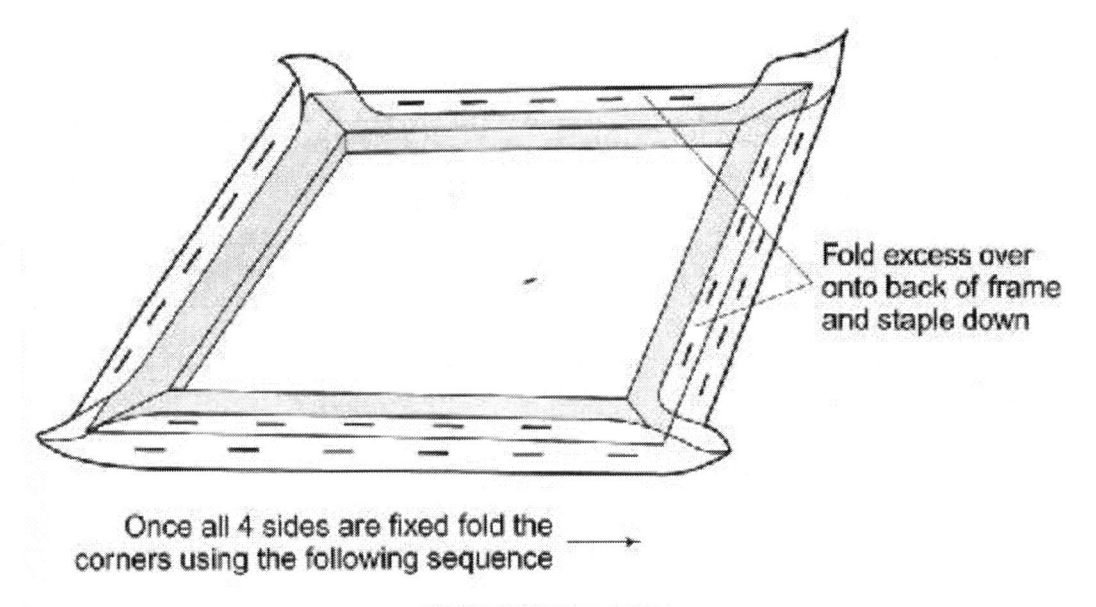

Fold excess over onto back of frame and staple down

Once all 4 sides are fixed fold the corners using the following sequence →

Fold and staple excess

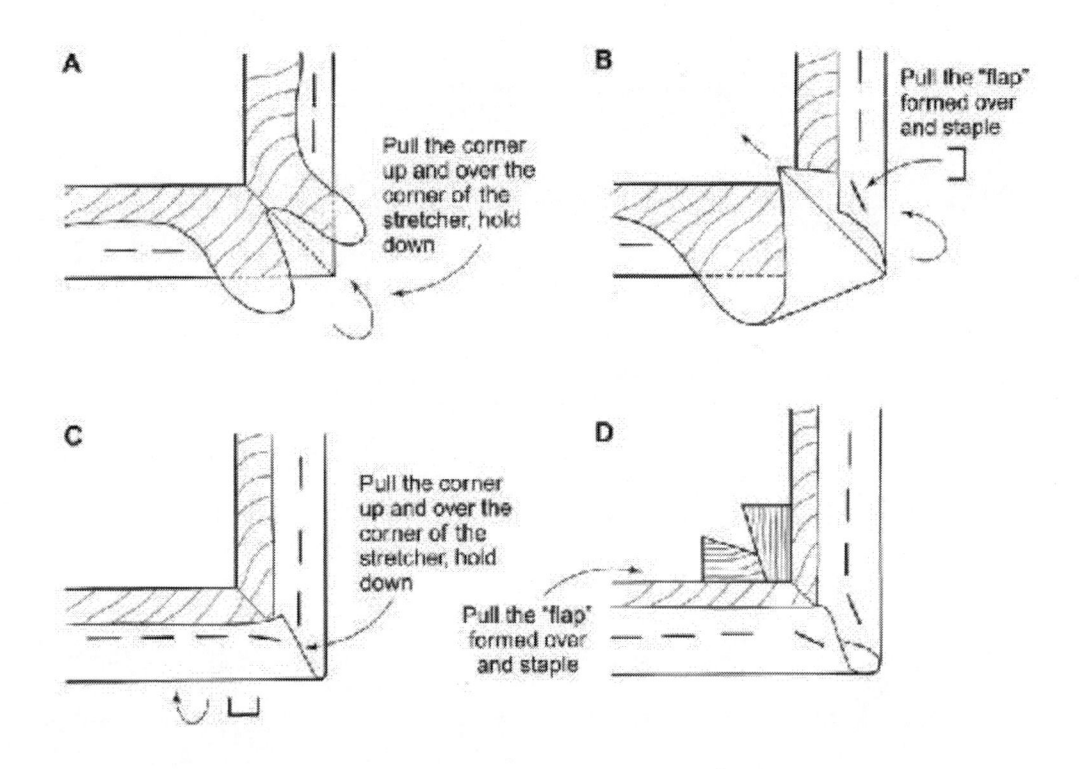

A Pull the corner up and over the corner of the stretcher, hold down

B Pull the "flap" formed over and staple

C Pull the corner up and over the corner of the stretcher, hold down

D Pull the "flap" formed over and staple

A+B, C+D corners fold and staple

Once again, get some canvas, some stretcher frames and practice - don't whatever you do use someone's precious picture to train yourself on. Once you have perfected the technique and can produce professional stretched canvases you can sell them to your artist customer with no risk of waste.

STRETCHING A CANVAS

1. Using a pair of canvas stretching pliers, pull taut and tap in tacks. Start from the middle and work to the corners.

2. This is a painting being re-stretched - use the original holes where possible to maintain integrity of canvas.

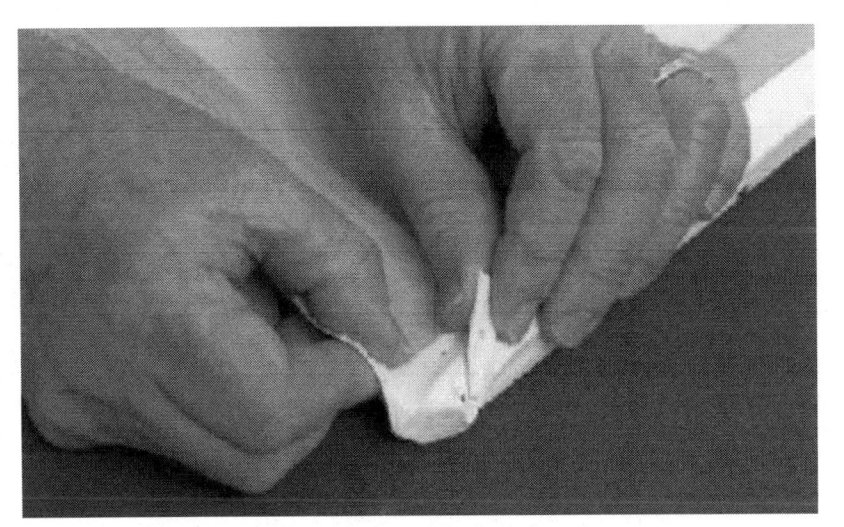

3 & 4. Fold corners carefully.

4.

5 & 6. Staple the back of the canvas flat.

6.

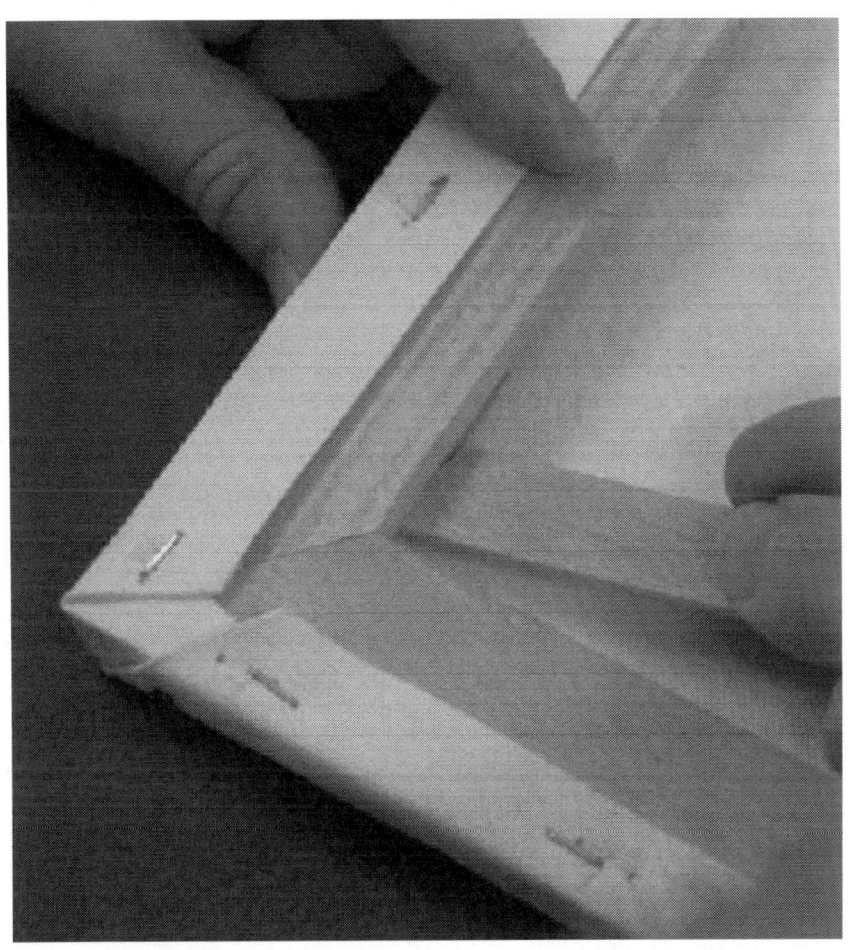

7, 8, 9, 10. Tap in wedges - work on opposite sides and be careful not to over stretch.

8.

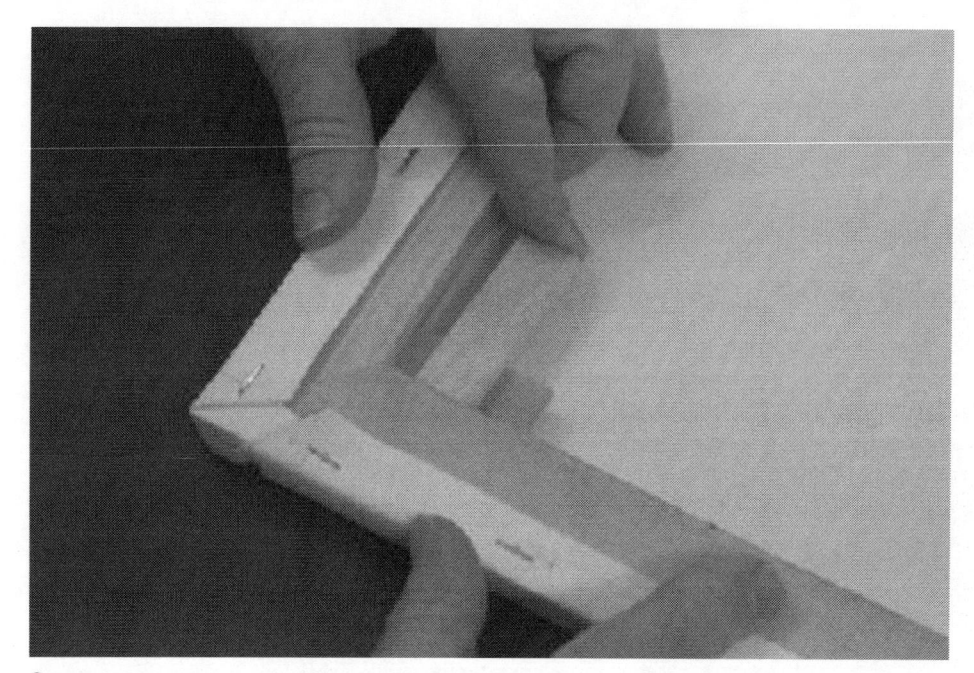

9.

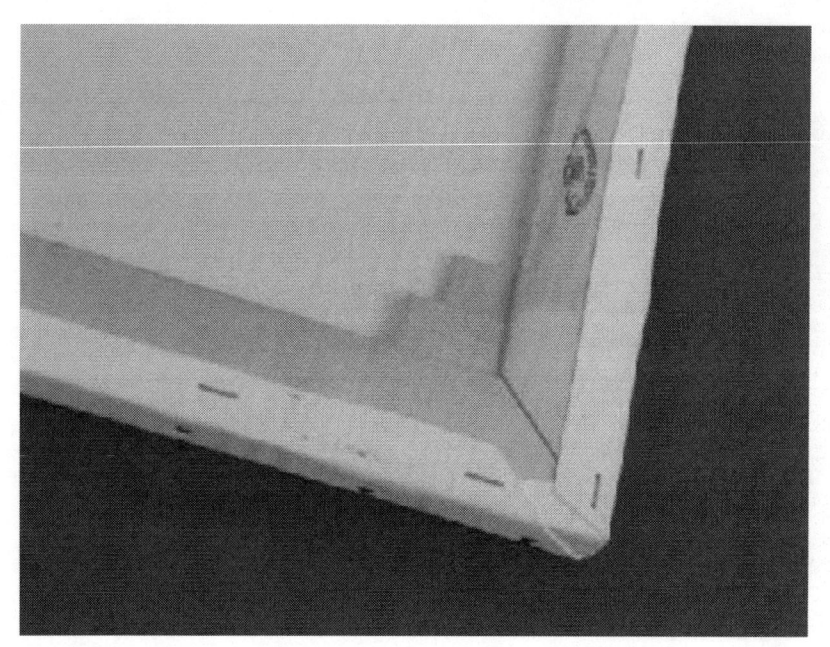

10.

11. The wedged and stretched canvas.

STRETCHING WATERCOLOURS

Some customers will request their watercolours be stretched. You will see many artists stretch their paper onto a board before painting. This is simply a method of moistening, not soaking, the back of the paper then taping the paper to a backing board using paper gum strip tape (NEVER synthetic tape) and allowing the whole to dry. The paper which expanded upon wetting shrink dries and the tape holds it to tension the paper making it taut. This is normally used when framing a badly "cockled" watercolour.

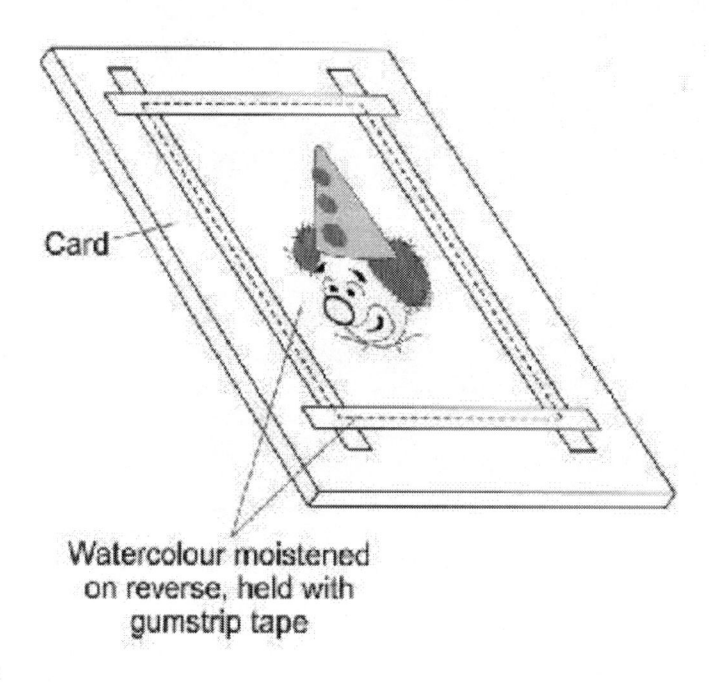

Card

Watercolour moistened on reverse, held with gumstrip tape

Stretching a watercolour.

STRETCHING A WATERCOLOUR

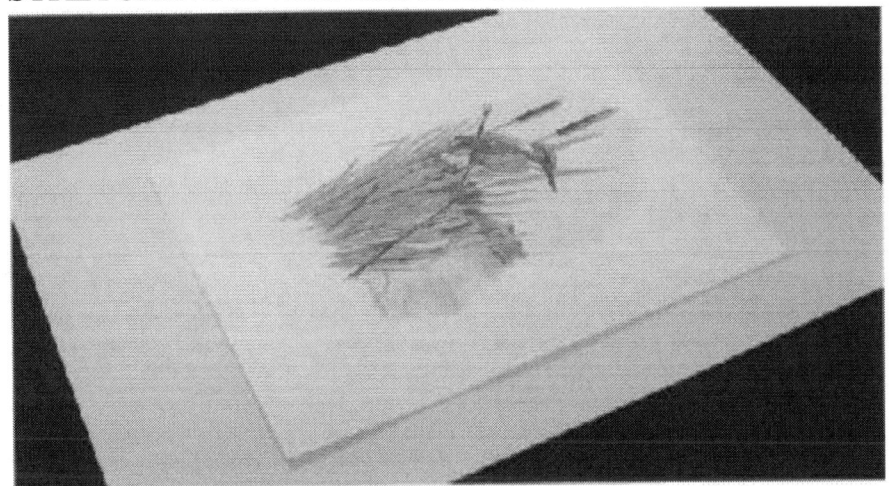

1. Watercolour to be stretched on its acid free backing board (trimmed to size)

2, 3 & 4. Cut strips of gum tape for all four sides.

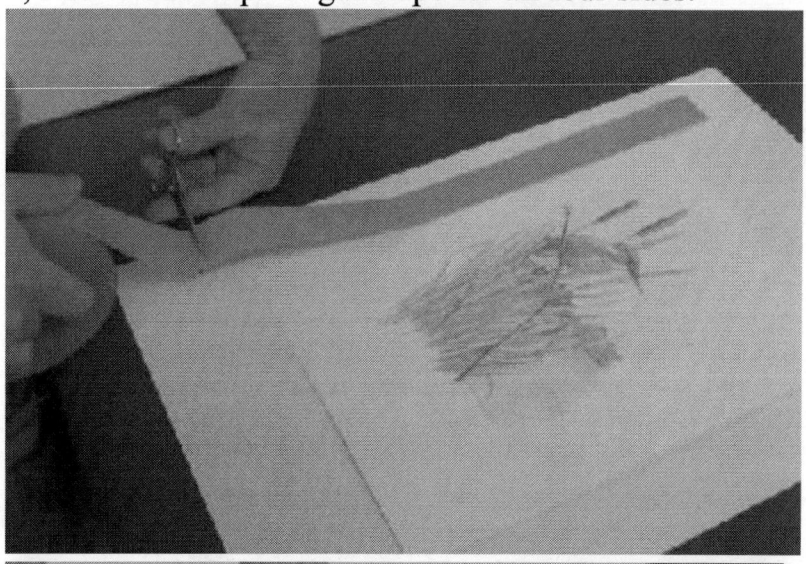

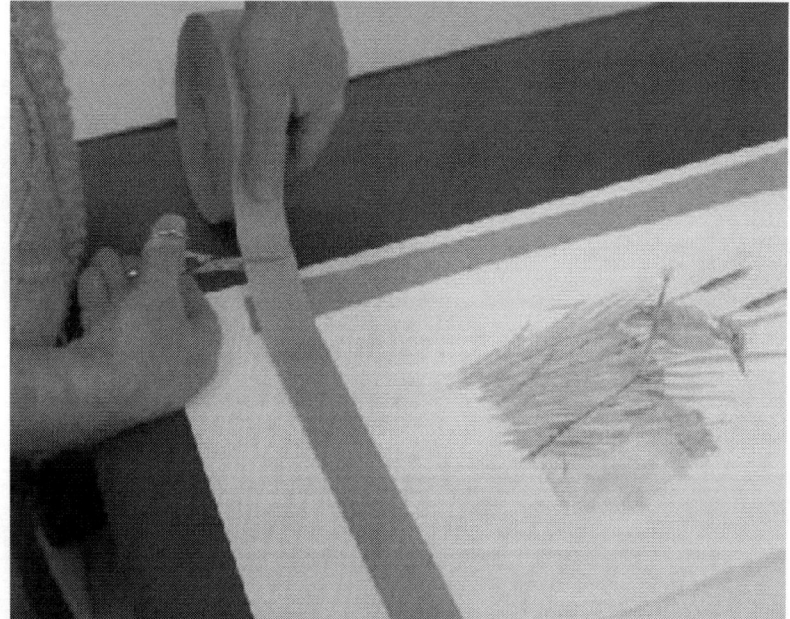

3.

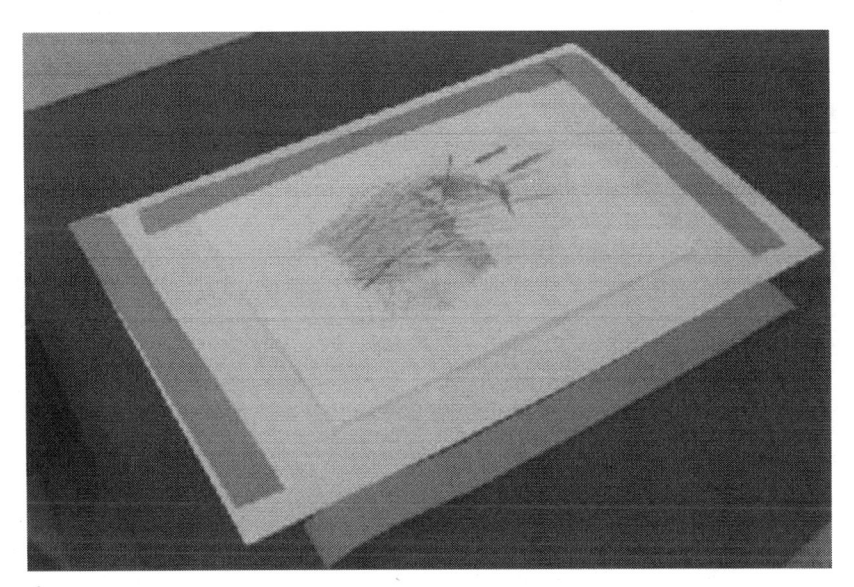

4.

5. Moisten the reverse of the watercolour (DO NOT OVERWET!!)

6. Wet the four lengths of tape

7 & 8. Lay the picture on the backing and tape along the edges. Leave to dry overnight.

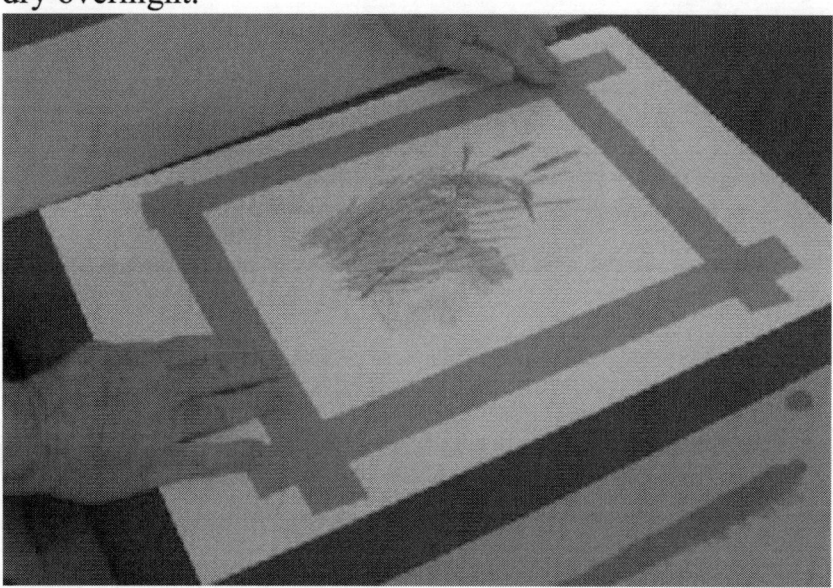

8.

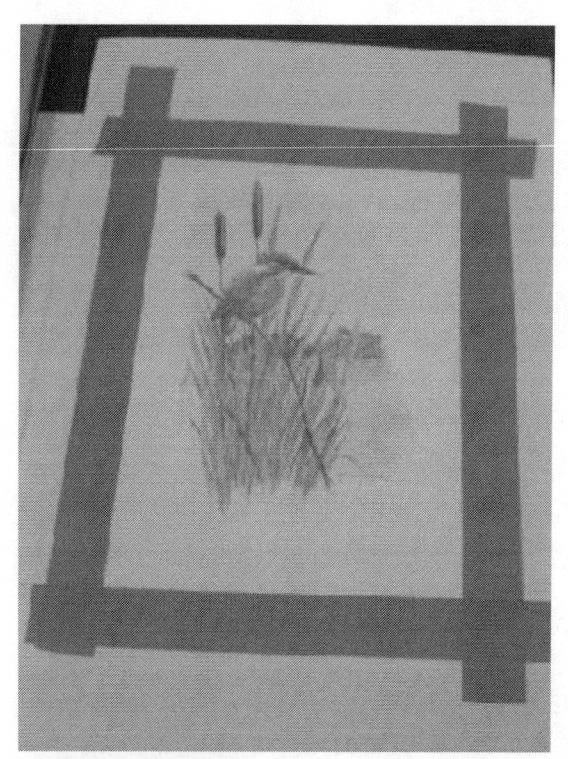

9. The stretched, smooth watercolour.

DRUMMING

Drumming is the stretching of a picture executed on sheep/calf skin vellum. It entails, like stretchingwatercolours, the moistening of the rear of the vellum then folding and taping the edges over a wood panel and allowing to dry. Once again, be very careful not to split the vellum, or over tension and bend or break the backing board. This is a process now so rare that you might never need it but it is worth knowing what to do!

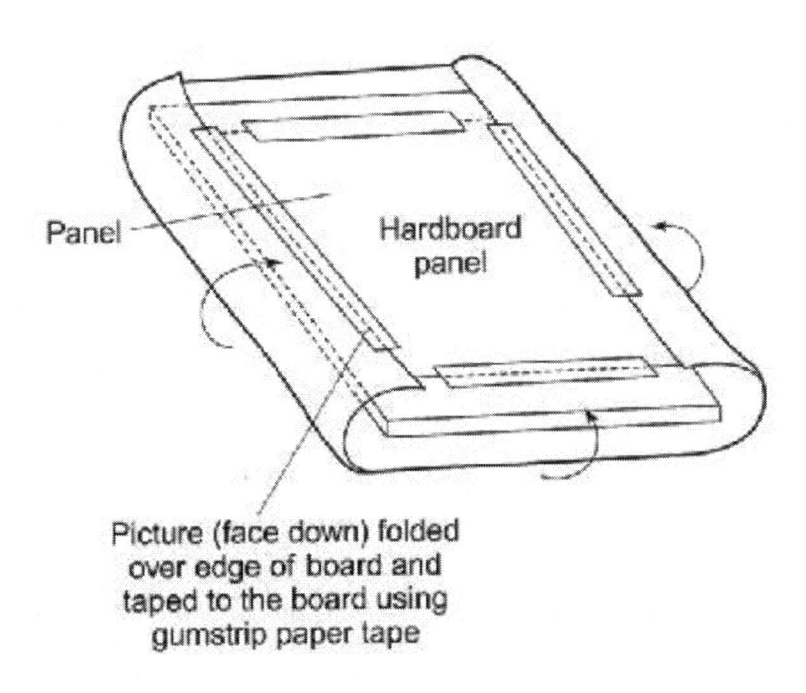

Panel

Hardboard panel

Picture (face down) folded over edge of board and taped to the board using gumstrip paper tape

'Drumming' - stretching a sheepskin vellum

DRY MOUNTING

Many framers now use dry mounting which is basically the sticking down of a picture using a sheet of "resin" glue which is heated to become adhesive, bonding the picture to the backing. You often see photographs in windows that are on framed canvas like an oil painting - that is dry mounted. To get the picture flat requires a vacuum press - a glass top box from which the air is extracted. The vacuum pulls the picture, resin and backing together perfectly flat and the press heats the resin at the same time, causing it to bond the whole into a sandwich. This process also bonds on a clear plastic covering film on top of the picture.

I have never used dry mounting and never had a demand for it. The suppliers on the other hand supply pre-glued cold mounting board, where the glue is covered by a film of wax paper. It works very well for sticking pictures down flat.

To prevent air bubbles, use as follows:

Cut the board slightly larger than the picture and place on the bench. From the bottom edge of the board, lift up and peel back about 40cm (1½in.) of the covering paper and fold down flat. Carefully align and stick the bottom edge of the picture to the exposed board, then with one hand between the board and picture, grip the cover paper and with the other hand using a *clean* lino printing roller, peel the cover paper whilst at the same time rolling the picture flat. Keep going until you reach the top edge. This method should stick the picture down without air bubbles. Trim the board down to size.

Once again practice on old prints and paper before attempting the operation on your customer's picture. A tip on this is should you get an air bubble, flatten by pricking the picture with a fine pin and rolling down flat, allowing the air to escape. With care this can be invisibly done but it is much better not to get air bubbles in the first place.

KRAFT PAPER BACKING

On the theme of stretching, in some parts of the world it is fashionable to cover the back of the frame with Kraft paper. To do this, cut a piece of Kraft paper to fit loosely over the backing board. Moisten the back and stick on with gum strip paper tape. The Kraft paper held to the frame by the gum strip will stretch and give, when dry, a drum skin taut backing.

GUM STRIP TAPING

To prevent the ingress of dust or insects in the frame via the fine crack between moulding rebate and glass, you should tape the inside of the rebate and the glass with gum strip tape.

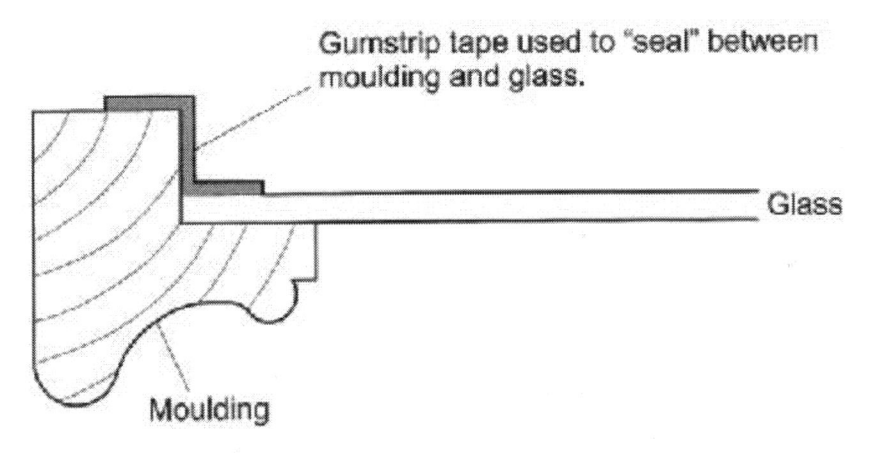

Gum-strip taping

FIRE SCREEN

Fire screens are in effect a picture frame with a top handle and a pair of feet screwed on.

I have seen various designs of fire screen fittings at Framing Wholesalers but the best I have found have come from Sundries Wholesalers. These are firms that supply the cabinet making and carpentry trades. The one I have always used is "Frank B Scraggs".

One of the differences between a fire screen and a hanging frame is the back finishing. You do not tape up the rear, rather put the hardboard or MDF back panel in place and cover the moulding/backing joint with a wood strip or thin plank.

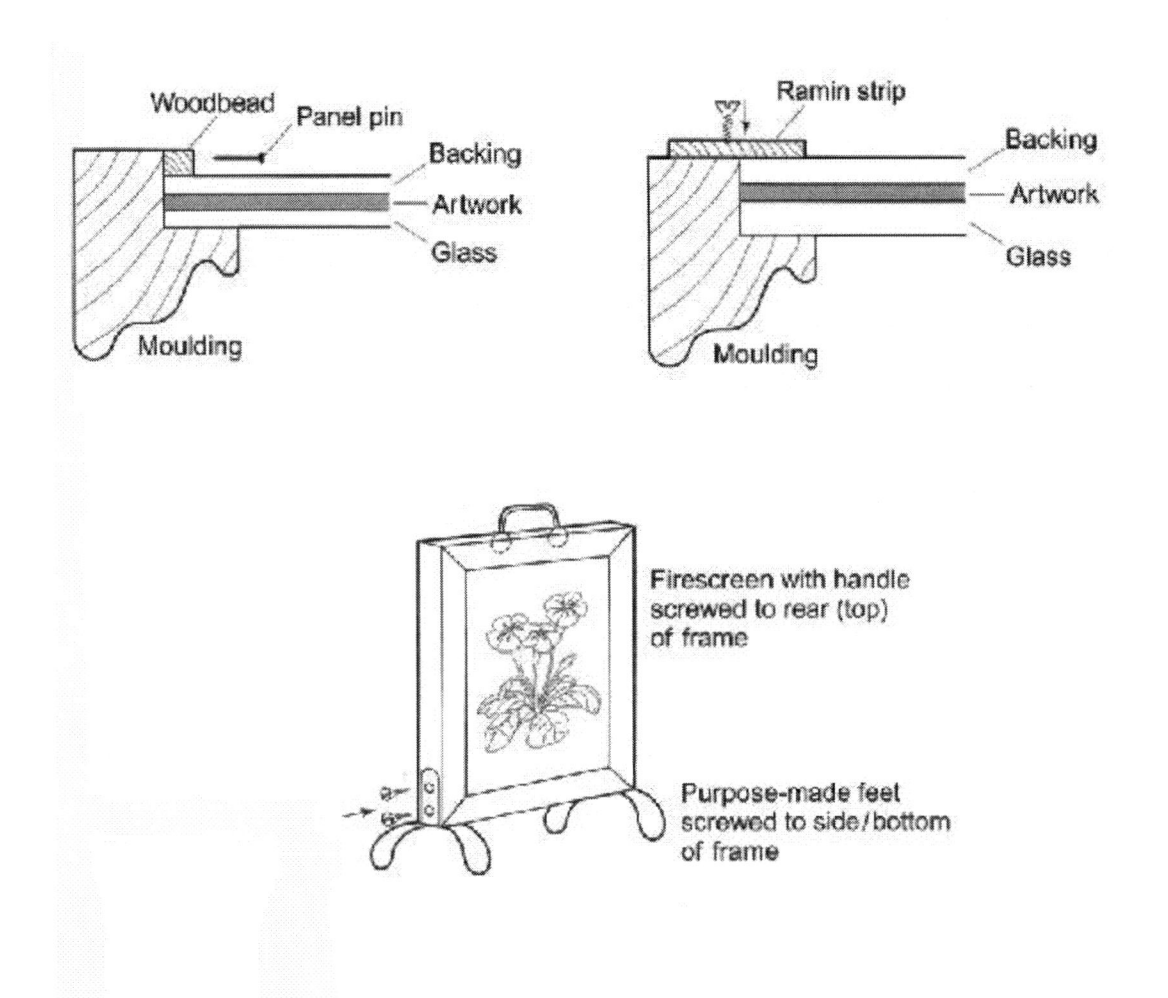

Finishing the back of a fire screen

Box frames make good fire screens with artificial flower arrangements, plates, small carpets, tapestries - the scope is endless.

GILDING

Gilding is the process whereby a surface is covered in some form of metallic leaf, called leaf because it comes in very fine sheet form, usually in a book to separate the individual sheets.

This includes gold leaf, where sheets of pure gold leaf usually in books of 25 sheets approximately 80 x 80mm square and .001mm thick, so fine in fact that it blows away and crumples on the slightest draught.

It is picked up using a "Gilder's Tip". This in effect is a fine flat brush made of badger hair. Brush your face with this to pick up some "skin oil" or static, to help the leaf stick and transfer it to a guilder's pad or cushion - a pad made with fine animal skin (calf or pig). The leaf is cut to size using a guilder's knife, then placed onto the work piece and "tamped" into place using fine soft hair (usually sable) brushes or mops before using "agate" burnishers to rub the leaf to produce a high shine. Small pieces of leaf can be applied using your finger. Once again, wipe your finger down the outside(!) of your nose to grease it before picking up the pre-cut fragment and placing it where you want it.

Aside from the leaf in book form mentioned above, there exists a variety of gold leaf that is pressed into the surface of fine paper, making handling much easier. It is applied in a similar way to plastic picture transfers. Apart from gold leaf there are imitation gold and silver leafs made of metal alloys which are produced in larger sheet form and are somewhat easier to apply. However, these will tarnish if not protected. Such protection used to be achieved by coating the leaf with shellac or wax but now, more often than not, acrylic varnish is used. Lastly there are the gilt paints and creams or wax pastes. These are mainly used for "making good" your moulding spine, i.e., where the pin holes or clamp marks are visible. Gold paint and waxes do not produce the sort of finish effects you get on professional frames.

Preparing your surface for gilding

If it is an old frame, and you intend to completely guild it, clean off the old gilt. For this, I use 20 grams of bicarbonate of soda with the same amount of detergent in 1 litre of water, stirred well and rubbed onto the surface with a piece of sponge. Then rub with a toothbrush to remove any stubborn gilt. Wipe off and rinse with methylated spirits then rub smooth. Fine wire wool formed round a stick like an "ear bud" is useful. Having cleaned your frame, make sure it is in good condition. Fill in holes, cracks, chips, etc. As with making good new frames, I use Brummers Interior Stopping for this task - I have yet to find anything as good!

For gilding you will then have to apply gesso. (Please note that the polymer based product used on artists canvases and called "gesso" is not the same product.)

Apply gesso in thin coats and when dry, smooth. This is repeated up to 12 coats. The gesso can be tinted with dry pigment, usually dark burnt sienna. This prepared surface is then coated in Size. This is usually called "Bole" and is a fine clay, usually coloured red. Several coats are applied. Allow to dry and using the finest abrasive and very gentle pressure, smooth - but do not rub through - the red coats.

Mix up a Guilder's liquor - I use a teacup into which I put seven parts distilled water with three parts methylated spirits mixed well. Paint this onto the surface and wait until it has become tacky. (Place a knuckle of a bent finger onto the surface and lift it away. If it releases with a "click", the surface is ready for the leaf.) Once gilded do not touch for 12 hours then polish gently with a piece of cotton wool, or if you wish to burnish, wait 6 hours before burnishing the gold leaf surface with an agate burnisher. Work slowly and thoroughly.

A few hints on gilding

1. Do not wear clothes that carry a static charge.

2. To reduce the sheet size of your leaf, take 3 or 4 leaves between their tissues and tear into quarters. Do not cut as you will damage or crimp the edges. These can be used in small areas.

3. Let your sheets overlap by 2-3mm and let them down gently onto the size but do not let fingers, or gilder's tip, touch the size.

4. Do not attempt to get gold leaf into inaccessible areas. They are normally painted after with liquid gilt.

5. Varnish is not necessary over gold leaf unless to age the frame.

Gilding is a difficult, time consuming process that is very expensive and takes a lot of practice to perfect. I have never found a commercial demand for it in a normal day to day picture framing business, but it is worth looking at as your business grows and you look for more directions to expand in.

I left gilding well alone for a long time. It was only when I had a successful picture framing business that I diversified to the more specialised services. Incidentally, book binding is a craft that fits in with framing if you have got the space - but that's another story!

PICTURE RESTORATION

This is a line of framing I have always avoided. Many framers do picture restoration and I have seen more pictures ruined then enhanced unless carried out by a professional.

Picture restoration is a completely separate profession that requires training, experience and great skill. Highly skilled separate profession that takes training, experience and great skill. Your local museum, or Council Gallery (or failing that one of the major City Museums) will probably furnish you with a list of restorers. I got the name of a restorer from an Art Auctioneers and always refer restoration to that source.

If you really want to go in to restoration, study the skill and if necessary take lessons - do it properly! Picture frame restoration is an easier option. If you master Guiding, frame restoration is fairly straight forward but bear in mind that with the mass produced moulding of the last 50 years, it is probably easier to make a new frame. Old wood frames can be cleaned and re-polished (remember some may have been distressed and antiquated on purpose!) and basic frame damage - chips, scratches and sprung mitres - is fairly easy to repair. The mitres can be easily rejoined, scratches and chips filled and colour matched and camouflaged - see the section on making good in Professional/Semi-professional Framing.

A customer of mine once brought some beautiful old prints in rosewood frames to me that he had found in an attic. The glass was scratched and beyond repair so I replaced the glass, cut new "museum" quality mounts and backing and lightly boot polished the frames. The end result was stunning and much appreciated.

USING OFF-CUTS

Whenever I have a quantity of assorted off-cuts of moulding, glass, mount board, etc., I make up small frames (miniatures) that will take postcards or greeting cards and illustrations (a good way of recycling Christmas/birthday cards). Displayed in my workshop, these little pictures always sell as fast as I can produce them, effectively turning waste into profit. You can also use them with mirror off-cuts to make small mirrors - always popular.

You can use mount board off-cuts with the same frames, plus make up assorted mounts and display them at cut price for the local artists.

Glass remnants that are unusable can (should rather) be taken to the local glass recycling centre. They now sell gadgets that break up your glass waste to fine waste but I still prefer to recycle mine.

CONCLUSION

Uniquely, picture framing is an Art, a Craft and a Trade. It is a service to a community and, like plumbers and electricians, good picture framers will always be In demand,

Picture framing Itself Is a lucrative and immensely satisfying occupation that combines the technical, mechanical and artistic side of a person's nature, It is easy to start as it does not require permits or licences and for this picture framer it has produced many years of interest and satisfaction - I have seen the most incredible artwork and pictures, met interesting people and had the intense pleasure of being my own boss.

Even on a 'hobby' basis, to be able to frame pictures or other objects yourself, or as an artist, your own work, to a standard and presentation of your choice can greatly enhance the satisfaction of ownership or creation. In this book I have tried to give you all the hints, tips and knowledge I have learned over the last 30 years of picture framing and whether you are interested in just framing your own work or in having a hobby that can also earn its keep or whether you wish to become a full time professional framer,

I sincerely hope you find it useful.

Happy Framing!

Made in the USA
Columbia, SC
24 January 2025